A Charles Olson Reader

CHARLES OLSON was born in 1910 in Worcester, Massachusetts and grew up there, spending summers in Gloucester, a seaport north of Boston. He studied at Harvard, and taught there for a time, before working for the Roosevelt government during the war. In 1948 he took a post at Black Mountain College, North Carolina, where as rector from 1951 to 1956 he was instrumental in attracting a circle of creative artists to the college. In 1958 he returned to live in Gloucester, the setting of the *Maximus Poems* (1960-68). His important books include his essay 'Projective Verse' (1950), which influenced poets such as Robert Duncan, Denise Levertov and Robert Creeley, *In Cold Hell, In Thicket* (1953), and his critical work *Call Me Ishmael* (1947). Charles Olson died in 1970.

RALPH MAUD had his early schooling in Yorkshire. After study at Harvard, he spent his first working years in Buffalo, where he published an edition of *The Notebooks of Dylan Thomas*. His work on Thomas includes *Entrances to Dylan Thomas' Poetry* (1963), the bibliography *Dylan Thomas in Print* (1970) and new editions with Walford Davies of Thomas's *Collected Poems* (1988) and *Under Milk Wood* (1995).

Ralph Maud was a colleague of Charles Olson's at the State University of New York at Buffalo for two years. He has taken on the task of assembling a replica of Olson's library in anticipation of restoring Olson's home at 28 Fort Square, Gloucester, Massachusetts as a research centre for Olson studies. He is the author of *Charles Olson's Reading: A Biography* (1996) and, as Emeritus Professor of English at Simon Fraser University and Associate of the Institute of Humanities there, has edited the *Selected Letters of Charles Olson* (2000).

Charles Olson, photographed by Renate Gerhardt in Germany, December 1966. The Kate Olson Archive.

A Charles Olson Reader

edited with an introduction by

Ralph Maud

CARCANET

First published in Great Britain in 2005 by
Carcanet Press Limited
Alliance House
Cross Street
Manchester M2 7AQ

Works by Charles Olson copyright © The University of Connecticut Libraries
and © The Estate of Charles Olson 2005
Introduction, selection and editorial matter copyright © Ralph Maud 2005

The right of Ralph Maud to be identified as the editor of this work has been asserted
by him in accordance with the Copyright, Designs and Patents Act of 1988
All rights reserved

A CIP catalogue record for this book is available from the British Library
ISBN 1 85754 784 5

The publisher acknowledges financial assistance from Arts Council England

Typeset by XL Publishing Services, Tiverton
Printed and bound in England by SRP Ltd, Exeter

Contents

Introduction	ix
List of Abbreviations and References	xiv

I Prologue — 1
La Préface — 2
The Resistance (for Jean Riboud) — 3

II Parents — 5
The Post Office — 6
As the Dead Prey Upon Us — 24

III Projective Verse — 32
The Kingfishers — 32
Projective Verse — 39

IV Maximus (1): Polis — 50
Letter 3 — 51
The Songs of Maximus — 55
Letter 10 — 59
Capt Christopher Levett (of York) — 63
Maximus to Gloucester, Letter 27 [withheld] — 67

V In Thicket — 70
La Chute — 70
In Cold Hell, in Thicket — 72
The Ring of — 77

VI Outside the Box — 79
The Gate & the Center — 79
from Mayan Letters — 86
To Gerhardt, There, Among Europe's Things… — 102
Human Universe — 112
Variations Done for Gerald Van De Wiele — 123

VII Maximus (2): Cosmology — 129
Letter #41 [broken off] — 130
MAXIMUS, FROM DOGTOWN – I — 131

MAXIMUS, FROM DOGTOWN – II	138
The Poimanderes	143
I forced the calm grey waters	143
A Maximus Song	144
Maximus, at the Harbor	145
A Later Note on / Letter #15	147
'View': fr the Orontes / fr where Typhon	148
after the storm was over	150
3rd letter on Georges, unwritten	151
to enter into their bodies	152
The Cow of Dogtown	153
Gylfaginning VI	157
All night long	158
[MAXIMUS, FROM DOGTOWN – IV]	158
VIII Causal Mythology	166
from Causal Mythology	166
IX Maximus (3): Earthly Paradise	186
having descried the nation	186
Maximus to himself June 1964	187
Cole's Island	188
Maximus of Gloucester	191
[to get the rituals straight	192
Celestial evening, October 1967	194
* Added to making a Republic	196
I'm going to hate to leave this Earthly Paradise	197
The first of morning was always over there	204
I live underneath the light of day	205
Appendix: 'Maximus, to himself'	207
TYRE	208
from 'Paris Review Interview'	209
Notes	213

Illustrations

Charles Olson, photographed by Renate Gerhardt
in Germany, December 1966. The Kate Olson Archive.   Frontispiece

Corrado Cagli, *Buchenwald 3*, 1945. Courtesy of the Charles Olson
Society.   1

The Olson family at Stage Fort Park, Gloucester, c. 1918. Photograph
courtesy of the University of Connecticut Libraries, Storrs.   5

Charles Olson with his father in his post office uniform, c. 1911.
Kate Olson Archive.   7

Gloucester, Mass.; view looking west from East Gloucester. Plate G
from 'The Fishermen of the United States' by George Brown
Goode and Joseph W. Collins, section IV of George Brown Goode
(ed.), *The Fisheries and Fishery Industries of the United States*
(US Commission of Fish and Fisheries, Washington DC:
Government Printing Office 1887).   50

The ichthyologist J.L.B. Smith and coelacanth, from a
contemporary newspaper article, c. December 1952.   55

Cover of *The Maximus Poems* (New York: Jargon/Corinth 1960),
showing map of Gloucester, Mass.   60

Figures from Stela D, Copan, Yucatan.   111

Olson's *casa* in Lerma, Yucatan, viewed from the beach.
Photograph courtesy of Bryant Knox.   122

Farewell party for Stefan Wolpe, Black Mountain College 1956.
Photographs courtesy of Gerald Van De Wiele.   124

Cover of *Maximus Poems IV, V, VI* (London: Cape Goliard 1968).   129

Diana of Ephesus, from Erich Neumann's *The Great Mother* (1955).   137

Nut supported by Shu, and the sun in its course.   157

Cover of the Four Seasons Foundation *Causal Mythology* (1969),
showing Olson at the blackboard, Berkeley Poetry Conference,
July 1965.   185

Figure of the Madonna cradling a ship, on the roof of the
Portuguese church of Our Lady of Good Voyage, Gloucester,
Mass. Photograph courtesy of the Charles Olson Society.   188

Mary B. Mellen, *Moonlight on a Bay* (Gloucester Harbor, 1870s; formerly attributed to Fitz Hugh Lane). Copyright © Shelburne Museum, Shelburne, Vermont. 197

Interior of 28 Fort Square, c. 1968. Photograph courtesy of the Charles Olson Society. 198

Olson's kitchen table, c. 1968. Kate Olson Archive. 198

Facsimilies

'La Chute', 25 May 1949. Copyright © the University of Connecticut Libraries, 2005. 71

'TYRE': draft of 'Maximus, to himself', April 1953. Copyright © the University of Connecticut Libraries, 2005. 208

Introduction

Charles Olson's first book, *Call Me Ishmael*, published by Reynal and Hitchcock in New York in 1947, was reprinted by Grove Press in 1958, by City Lights in 1967 (also by Jonathan Cape in London the same year), and is now, in a facsimile of the first printing, kept in print by Johns Hopkins University Press (1997). That Olson's reputation as a pioneer Melville scholar is secure signals that there might be no harm in leaving that role of Olson's aside and, as far as this *Reader* is concerned, attending to the rest of what he has to offer.

In introducing an anthology designed for an audience other than his own countrymen it might be appropriate to remember how much Olson, though acknowledgedly an archetypal American, has looked abroad for sources and support. All his grandparents came from Europe, Sweden on his father's side, Ireland on his mother's. In the summer of 1928, at the age of eighteen, he did a version of the Grand Tour. This came as a prize for distinguishing himself in an international oratory contest. The group stayed in Oxford, Paris, Amsterdam, Milan and Venice, with Olson breaking away on his own for a side trip to Rome.

He did not get to Europe again until 1965, but consider the following connections. His first book of poems *y & x* (1948) was in collaboration with the Italian artist Corrado Cagli and was published by Caresse Crosby's Black Sun Press (Paris and Washington). His second book *In Cold Hell, in Thicket* (1953) was put out by Robert Creeley from Majorca, as was *Mayan Letters* (1953). *The Maximus Poems 1–10* (1953) and *The Maximus Poems 11–22* (1956) were both printed in Stuttgart by Jonathan Williams while he was serving there as a US soldier. Jean-Paul Sartre picked up a Melville piece for *Les Temps Moderne* (October 1951). Rainer Gerhardt featured Olson in his *fragmente* (1951) and *Ferrini & Others* (1955). There was a French *Appelez-Moi Ismaël* (1962) and a German *Gedichte* (1965). Elaine Feinstein published Olson in *Prospect* (1960) while she was at Cambridge; one of Olson's seminal essays was written as 'Letter to Elaine Feinstein' (1959). A voluminous correspondence with Jeremy Prynne began in 1961; as a guest editor he published Olson in *Prospect* in 1964. Prynne's students featured Olson in *Granta* (1964), *Wivenhoe Park Review* (1965) and *Resuscitator* (1964). *The Review* 'Black Mountain' issue edited by Charles Tomlinson (January 1964) featured Olson.

In June 1965 Olson was invited by Gian Carlo Menotti to the Festival of Two Worlds in Spoleto. Following that, he went to the PEN conference in Bled, Yugoslavia. He was invited to read in Berlin in December 1966, and stayed for an extended period in London, eventually going down to Dorchester for three weeks to research the Weymouth Port Books and the records of the voyages which founded Gloucester, Massachusetts. On 12 July 1967 he appeared in the International Poetry Festival at the Albert Hall.

That was the climax of his two jet-set years, but the connections he made with British poets such as Tom Raworth led to publications from Goliard Press (London): first the beautiful small pamphlet *'West'* (1966) and then the major *Maximus Poems IV, V, VI* (with Cape, 1968). These publications from London provided great momentum to Olson's career. To them should be added the posthumous editions, among others *The Maximus Poems* (1983), *Collected Poems* (1987), *Collected Prose* (1997) and *Selected Letters* (2000), all from the University of California Press.

I hope the above account has begun to suggest Olson's status as a substantial poet of his time. Some consider him pre-eminently such, because of the 'Projective Verse' essay – very liberating to younger poets – and because of the epic range of the *Maximus Poems* comparable to Pound's *Cantos* and William Carlos Williams's *Paterson*. (Olson acknowledged these forebears but fought to claim a separate vision and modality.) What should also be brought into account is the energy and humour which Olson carried with him into company anywhere and which endeared him in a very deep way to friends and acquaintances.

I knew Olson in Buffalo when he joined the faculty of the university for two years from 1963 to 1965. I had been born and educated in Yorkshire, England, and came to America in 1949 full of Philip Larkin, Kingsley Amis, John Wain and other university wits. At Harvard I moved among the intellectual poets of the New England tradition, Richard Wilbur, Donald Hall and others who drew from Robert Frost. All this changed when I was presented with Olson's genius. He put before us a contrary path which still seems viable to me twenty-five years after his death, and which the present volume hopes to make attractive to the reader.

No matter what strengths a collection of Olson's works might have, it will always fall short in one regard: the portrayal of the extraordinary momentum of life which produced it. As Jeremy Prynne once put it, referring to Olson's *Maximus IV, V, VI* in a lecture:

> The poem is simple, but the life it came out of, and the pre-occupations that surround it, immeasurably dense and confused and packed with a kind of fertile obscurity... The man had to have around him a great mass of dense information and confusion, a great mass of pressure, from

which at any moment he could spring out another section of the work. (*Minutes* #28, p. 5)

Some sense of this can be felt in the example of a poem that never actually got done because of the special kind of 'confusion' surrounding it. 'That missing poem', Olson told an audience at Goddard College,

> is a story I may not be competent to write, but it should be a story which I know a man who wrote – I'm involved in that problem: shall I crib him or not? Very great writer, who won the running broad jump at the first modern Olympics in Athens: James Connolly. What I'd like to do is what he can do and has done, which is to take a vessel from the eastern end of Georges shoal, the north-eastern end, and run it at night in an easterner and eastward through the maze of the shoals of the north end of Georges without wrecking, and getting into clear water on the other side, and making the market in Boston. (*Minutes* #2, p. 26)

I like the mention of the running broad jump at the first modern Olympics, not impertinent to a discussion of proprioception. Olson is thinking of the chapter in James L. Connolly's *The Book of the Gloucester Fishermen* (New York 1927) called 'Driving Home from Georges', where Maurice Whalen, captain of *The Binney* with Connolly as passenger, did exactly the 'cuttin' the corner off the North Shoal' that Olson is talking about. Connolly writes:

> Let no reader imagine that Maurice Whalen was a foolish sort. That drive home from Georges was about as desperate a passage as he ever made; yet I felt safer with him than I have with unskilled amateurs once or twice in moderately smooth water. Whalen knew his vessel, knew what she could do and could not do in wind and sea. (pp. 138–9)

It was, we should remind ourselves, the skill and courage of such fishermen that provided the measure for everything that Olson touched upon, politics, scholarship, poems. Listen to Olson talking in an interview (*Muthologos* 2.165–6) about Louis Douglas, the fisherman who, he says, 'made me a poet simply because of the nature of his language when I listened behind a stone wall to him and his brother from Newfoundland talk when I was four years old'. Douglas visited him on Fort Point after a gap of some years:

> ... when he walked in he wasn't going to stop, but then he saw my windows and he said, 'My lord, Charlie, you do have, you have some, you have a lot of windows looking out! I says, yes. So I said, come

through the house and see it. Sat down and talked for three hours, identified everything that ever was on the Fort. He has that fantastic condition of the human race when everything mattered. Today, nothing does, and that's what's so poor. And I know men for whom everything matters. Still! Who see, feel, and know that everything that they run into does matter. Hah! and then they retain it. And then they have it. And then they have it forever. And when they're buried they're bigger than those people who don't. Even if they look the same and fit the same box.

Which is where, indeed, the challenge is for Olson himself. So in '3rd letter on Georges, unwritten' he holds off. The result can be read in the body of the texts of this volume.

What we are trying to get a sense of here is the life behind the poetry, where the mass of pressure, as Prynne put it, pushes the writing out of 'fertile obscurity'. And what a relief it is to be in the presence of a poet who has got infinitely more going than actually gets written down and published. On 17 March 1966 Olson wrote to Jack Sweeney, founder of the Harvard Poetry Room, who had recorded Olson's reading there:

By the way, I have continued to pursue the matter of Connolly's 'papers' at Colby, and as soon as spring is farther advanced, intend to shoot up there, and have a look. (The fellow who is in charge of the Library – a Professor – indicates there are a good pile of mss, some unpublished, and I'd hate to miss anything which by any chance was as good as stuff he published.) Would you by any chance enjoy accompanying me? It's not a bad run, even if my car – a Chevrolet station-wagon 1956 – shouldn't be trusted. (*Selected Letters*, p. 352)

It has to be said: that trip up into New Hampshire, if it ever came off, I would have given a lot to have gone along.

No one has pinpointed it better than Albert Glover, who also knew Olson at Buffalo:

Olson was 'out there' existing in a scale and a dimension that was absolutely inspiring. Some of that condition comes through in his writing, but his presence was, to me, of more importance than all the poems no matter how much I read and love them. The poems, I think, are what was left over *after* Charles had done what he was doing. (*Minutes* #19, p. 5)

Olson said it another way in writing to thank Charles Tomlinson for the review of *Maximus IV, V, VI* in the *New Statesman* for 3 March 1961: 'The thing is, to have been spoken of as a person with traits' (letter, 1 April 1961, at Storrs). This present anthology aims to proffer a person with traits, a person with poems, yes, with prose, but also with *traits*, which are our most cherished recognitions.

I wish to pay tribute to Robert Creeley's edition of *Selected Writings of Charles Olson* (New York: New Directions 1966), which I have used as a classroom text for the decades of my teaching. While I have been unable not to include here many of Robert Creeley's choices, I have heeded his 'Last Word' (p. 280):

> There is never an end to such a selection as this, and I might well begin again, all over, making a very different choice. But I would, more usefully, invite the reader to that possibility.

I am indebted to Michael Schmidt of Carcanet Press for enabling me to take up that challenge. I have been able to include much material beyond 1966 and have, of course, exercised my own judgement throughout. I have added short introductory statements to each item of poetry and prose in order to supply a running commentary connecting the poet's work to his life.

I would like to dedicate this volume to Rutherford Witthus, whose unfailing courtesy as the presiding spirit over the Charles Olson Archive at the Thomas J. Dodd Research Center of the University of Connecticut Libraries has given me and others the confidence to undertake sustained work on the many manuscripts that were left at the time of Charles Olson's premature death in 1970.

Ralph Maud
Vancouver, 2005

Abbreviations and References

CO/CC	*Charles Olson and Cid Corman: Complete Correspondence, 1950-1964.* Ed. George Evans. 2 vols. Orono, Maine: National Poetry Foundation, 1987, 1991.
CO/FB	*Charles Olson and Frances Boldereff: A Modern Correspondence.* Ed. Ralph Maud and Sharon Thesen. Middletown, Conn.: Wesleyan University Press, 1999.
CO/RC	*Charles Olson and Robert Creeley: The Complete Correspondence.* Vols. 1-8 ed. George F. Butterick; vols. 9-10 ed. Richard Blevins. Santa Rosa, Calif.: Black Sparrow Press, 1980–96.
Collected Poems	*The Collected Poems of Charles Olson: Excluding the Maximus Poems.* Ed. George F. Butterick. Berkeley and Los Angeles: University of California Press, 1987.
Collected Prose	*Collected Prose.* Ed. Donald Allen and Benjamin Friedlander. Berkeley and Los Angeles: University of California Press, 1997.
Distances	*The Distances: Poems.* New York: Grove Press, 1960.
Guide	George F. Butterick. *A Guide to the Maximus Poems of Charles Olson.* Berkeley: University of California Press, 1978.
Human Universe	*Human Universe and Other Essays.* Ed. Donald Allen. San Francisco: Auerhahn Press, 1965; reprint, New York: Grove Press, 1967.
In Cold Hell	*In Cold Hell, In Thicket.* Mallorca: Divers Press, 1953.
Maximus Poems	*The Maximus Poems.* New York: Jargon/Corinth, 1960.
Maximus IV, V, VI	*Maximus Poems IV, V, VI.* London: Cape Goliard, 1968.
Mayan Letters	*Mayan Letters.* Ed. Robert Creeley. Mallorca; The Divers Press, 1953.
Minutes	*Minutes of the Charles Olson Society.* Vancouver, BC.
Muthologos	*Muthologos: The Collected Lectures and Interviews.* Ed. George F. Butterick. 2 vols. Bolinas, Calif.: Four Seasons, 1978, 1979.
Post Office	*The Post Office: A Memoir of His Father.* Ed. George F. Butterick. Bolinas, Calif.: Grey Fox Press, 1975.
Selected Letters	*Selected Letters.* Ed. Ralph Maud. Berkeley: University of California Press, 2000.
Selected Writings	*Selected Writings of Charles Olson.* Ed. Robert Creeley. New York: New Directions, 1966.
Stanford	Special Collections Library, Stanford University, Stanford.
Storrs	Special Collections Library, University of Connecticut, Storrs.
What Does Not Change	Ralph Maud. *What Does Not Change: The Significance of Charles Olson's 'The Kingfishers'.* Madison, N.J.: Fairleigh Dickinson University Press; London: Associated University Presses, 1998.
y & x	*y & x.* Paris: Black Sun Press, 1948.

I. Prologue

Two men – and Europeans at that – were significantly present at Olson's inauguration as a mature poet. Corrado Cagli, the artist, and Jean Riboud, a consummate corporation executive, brought to Olson (as he later put it) 'the grace of life, which is still yours, my dear Europe' (*Muthologos* 2.152). But more than that, they brought, each in his own person, the immediate history of war and holocaust.

Cagli exiled himself from Mussolini's Italy in 1938 at the age of twenty-eight. Olson, the same age, met him just before Cagli was to volunteer for the US army. It was a marathon talking session: '3 days, Gloucester, he not knowing English, I not Italian... 3 days, and all night long mostly. How? Don't know. Just did it, the two of us. Crazy. May, 1940' (*CO/RC* 3.132).

This gives us one fixed point in the poem 'La Préface', the pre-war world: 'I had air my lungs could breathe.' We jump then to May 1946, when Olson walked into Cagli's first post-war show in New York City. Again they talked, Olson full of his Bigmans poems that would be an updated Gilgamesh, Cagli already moving on to a new phase of polytopes and 'the fourth dimension'. But the talk was constrained by the intervening war years and the atrocities that had just come to light. Indeed, Cagli was one of the harbingers of the horror, for his company had been the first to enter

Corrado Cagli, *Buchenwald 3*, 1945. Courtesy of the Charles Olson Society.

Buchenwald. Before them as they talked were the dead bodies he had sketched quickly at that moment that changed the world.

Olson, who had not been able to write about the war because he 'knew not', was by these drawings made to know, and he immediately wrote 'La Préface' as literally a preface to the show's catalogue when it moved to Chicago.

Another friend, Jean Riboud, must also have had something to do with 'La Préface'. As a French partisan he had been captured and spent two years in Buchenwald. When he emerged he had tuberculosis and weighed ninety-six pounds. His brother is quoted as saying that Buchenwald made him 'very strong, very capable of resisting anything' (quoted by Ken Auletta in *The New Yorker* 'Profile', 6 June 1983, p. 59). When Olson met him in New York Riboud was on his way to becoming CEO of the most profitable corporation in the world.

'The job of the poet,' Olson wrote in a 1945 notebook (now in the Archive at Storrs) 'is to be destructive, to get rid of the dead past.' Olson took these two men as a model for how to step forward out of destruction; they were a measure of his artistic aims at the beginning of his career as a post-war poet.

La Préface

Responding specifically to Corrado Cagli's Buchenwald drawings, this poem is meant to be a preface to all the life to be created on the foundation of 'that compost of civilization' (as Olson put it in notes at the time). The dead are emotionally 'in the way', and we must close the parentheses ( ) in order to get the future born. But the Babe howls in the underground passage of its rebirth. That the poem draws on Blake for its resonant ending is an admission that it is incomplete in itself, depending on allusions, a preface only. But which poet of Olson's generation wrote as gravely about this epic moment on whatever size of canvas?

The dead in via
              in vita nuova
                        in the way
You shall lament who know they are as tender as the horse is.
You, do not you speak who know not.

        'I will die about April 1st...' going off
        'I weigh, I think, 80 lbs...' scratch
        'My name is NO RACE'   address

Has great eyes in his heart. Is one of the rare ones

I. PROLOGUE

Buchenwald   new Altamira cave
With a nail they drew the object of the hunt.

Put war away with time, come into space.
It was May, precise date, 1940. I had air my lungs could breathe.
He talked, via stones   a stick   sea rock   a hand of earth.
It is now, precise, repeat. I talk of Bigmans organs
he, look, the lines! are polytopes.
And among the DPs – deathhead
      at the apex
          of the pyramid.

Birth in the house is the One of Sticks, cunnus in the crotch.
Draw it thus: (   ) 1910 (
It is not obscure. We are the new born, and there are no flowers.
Document means there are no flowers
       and no parenthesis.

It is the radical, the root, he and I, two bodies
We put our hands to these dead.

The closed parenthesis reads: the dead bury the dead,
       and it is not very interesting.
Open, the figure stands at the door, horror his
and gone, possessed, o new Osiris, Odysseus ship.
He put the body there as well as they did whom he killed.

Mark that arm. It is no longer gun.
We are born not of the buried but these unburied dead
crossed stick, wire-led, Blake Underground

The Babe
   the Howling Babe

The Resistance (for Jean Riboud)

Olson wrote in a letter of 10 May 1949 to Ben Shahn: 'There is a fine friend by name of Jean Riboud, yes, French, Lyon, now NY, though soon back to France. Have known him some two years since he has been here. <u>Has great eyes in his heart. Is one of the rare ones</u>' (letter in Archives of American Art). This *short essay, a personal tribute, is also a talisman pointing the 'intolerable way' out of the war: one opposes to extermination one's sheer physical survival. In all simplicity Riboud once said of his concentration camp experience that 'in the presence of death there are the ones who fight and the ones who give up'. We are defined by our resistance; we rest in the consolations of materialism.*

This is eternity. This now. This foreshortened span.

Men will recognize it more easily (& dwell in it so) when we regain what the species lost how long ago: nature's original intention with the organism, that it live 130 years. Or so Bogomolets' researches into the nature of connective tissue seem to prove. True or not, with or without aid from his own biosis, man has no alternative: he accepts his mortal years as his eternity. It is the root act.

There are other aids. Time, for example, has been cut down to size, though I do not think that those who have come to the knowledge of now came here from that powerful abstraction space-time, no matter how its corrections of time reinforce the position.

Man came here by an intolerable way. When man is reduced to so much fat for soap, superphosphate for soil, fillings and shoes for sale, he has, to begin again, one answer, one point of resistance only to such fragmentation, one organized ground, a ground he comes to by a way the precise contrary of the cross, of spirit in the old sense, in old mouths. It is his own physiology he is forced to arrive at. And the way – the way of the beast, of man and the Beast.

It is his body that is his answer, his body intact and fought for, the absolute of his organism in its simplest terms, this structure evolved by nature, repeated in each act of birth, the animal: man; the house he is, this house that moves, breathes, acts, this house where his life is, where he dwells/ against the enemy, the beast.

Or the fraud. This organism now our citadel never was cathedral, draughty tenement of soul, was what it is: ground, stone, wall, cannon, tower. In this intricate structure are we based, now more certainly than ever (besieged, overthrown), for its power is bone muscle nerve blood brain a man, its fragile mortal force its old eternity, resistance.

II. Parents

In a rare autobiographical statement of 1952 published in *Collected Prose* as 'The Present Is Prologue', Olson says that he is of the 'heterogeneous present' rather than the 'homogeneity of the Founders':

> My father was born Karl Joseph Olson, in Sweden, and his name probably reflects a story in the family that they were Hungarians on my grandmother's side. He was carried to the States at five months. My mother was Mary Hines, and Yeats told me (on the grounds of my grandfather, who was the immigrant, 'born in Cork and brought up in Galway') that my mother's grand-aunt must have been his 'Mary Hines,' the beloved of the blind poet Raftery and 'the most beautiful woman in all Western Ireland.' It was rough on my mother when I found this out at 18 – my father and I never let her forget the fall from grace, that she was only the most beautiful woman in South Worcester, Mass.

One does not need more than this thumbnail sketch to sense the father's jovial joking nature, the mother's warmth at flattery. Our parents are our definers, says Olson, and concludes that 'the work of each of us is to find out the true lineaments of ourselves by facing up to the primal features of these founders who lie buried in us.'

The Olson family at Stage Fort Park, Gloucester, c. 1918. Photograph courtesy of the University of Connecticut, Storrs.

The Post Office

In a notebook entry of 8 March 1948 Olson wrote of his current undertaking: 'At least one course is clear – do this book on yr father without reference to culture – style, manner, tricks – do it on the level of mediocre humanitas' (quoted in Post Office *p. vii). Of the three chapters that Olson finished, 'Mr. Meyer' is perhaps too muted, 'Stocking Cap' swings over to the idyllic, but 'The Post Office' is a true median, the hero-worship of his father tempered with embarrassments and the 'cocoon' of the family exposed to broader issues of society. The central theme is again resistance: 'the resistance of a man', one who carried into battle the pentangle of 'courtesy, modesty, care, proportion, respect'. So we see that the field of conflict is larger than the post office of Worcester, Massachusetts.*

I said it was my father's stubbornness that killed him in the end. It was, and the trouble out of which his death came was born fourteen years earlier. In its birth he was right. The fight he put up was a just one.

I can date it that exactly because it was his determination to take me to the celebration at Plymouth of the 300th anniversary of the Pilgrim landing that aggravated the situation his superiors in the Post Office had provoked.

My father had requested and received permission to take his vacation the week of the pageant at Plymouth. He and I were to go, leaving my mother at home. It was to be our first big trip and he had planned it most carefully, for it was a major excursion for him as well, comparable only to his trip alone, before I was born, to Gettysburg.

That trip had also got him into trouble, but of another sort, less mortal. It was with my mother. As far as I could ever get the picture he surprised her by going off, so soon after their marriage, on a holiday of his own. This may be a little unfair to her. It may be that the running references to the trip that I heard the rest of the years my father was alive were nothing more than the taunts by which we remind ourselves as well as the other of experience we have not shared. It is a part of that play of jealousy which inhabits the intimate life as much as affection does.

I myself was satisfied with the trip as was, as I heard it from him and as I was reminded of it by the two small pitchers he had brought back for my mother, of a most delicate porcelain, with scenes on them. They set on the mantelpiece in the dining-room and erased for me the two hideous vases at each end of the shelf, fat cylinders of unglazed flowered glass which looked to me as ugly as legs without ankles. In fact I was so delighted in my father's taste in choosing the pitchers that they created in me a delight in the trip

II. PARENTS

Charles Olson with his father in his post office uniform, c. 1911. Kate Olson Archive.

which makes it more sweet in memory than any of my own.

But not my mother. His letters or the pitchers or her sure sense the trip was right for him precisely as it had been made never blotted out what also stood on the shelf of her mind. It never does. She had the greed we have, to know all that happens to the other person. Our imagination won't, in this circumstance, stay straight. It corrupts, and we go back and back, as greedy to know as we are fearful to know too much.

Maybe my mother made so much of their marriage trip to New York to offset this Gettysburg which followed hard on it. They arrived in a blizzard and stayed at the old Grand Central Hotel. One thing stood out that could be talked about and that my mother dwelt on with a blush. She had packed no button hook for her high shoes. My father had to go out in the storm and at that hour find some store open. He picked up their umbrella, one of the wedding presents, and when he stepped out into the snow he stepped, she delighted to put it, into a rice storm as well!

I was not ten when the Plymouth trip was planned but my father had long since got over to me his interest in the American past. Any boy brought up in New England had worn the high hat and square, buckled shoes at Thanksgiving plays at school and written a life of George Washington round and round an elm tree at Cambridge. My father had taken me several steps down from that.

I'm not sure his first service wasn't on the biography of General George. I was working on it at the kitchen table with my mother ironing by the stove and him across from me over a drawing board, probably finishing a black and white (he was at that time making up for the schooling he didn't get by shipping lessons to a correspondence institute of art in Minneapolis). The essay was too much for me and I suddenly threw it up in disgust. The gesture struck him with almost the same force as the dice of the parchesi box did the time I dished them into his face in my anger he had licked me. That time he chased me and would have whaled me had it not been for my mother's frantic fear. When he caught up with me by the set tubs he contented himself with a milder torture. He merely pulled my hair.

Over George Washington he was gentle and strong. He talked. And he made his point, the more easily, I suppose, because I knew how thoroughly he himself worked, over a drawing board or on our neighbors' boilers or their plumbing. I had already learned one trick from him, handing tools to him: you can swear your way through the dirtiest weather. As his assistant then I acquired almost as good a tongue as I was later to, from certain fishermen I know.

What he had to say about me and George Washington was: do it. And I did it. It took.

It is easy to figure out how old I was. The paper was read to the class but I was completely embarrassed, especially because of Margarite Luddon who had the seat in front of me, and such beeyootiful hair. All the 'of's,' the teacher wanted the class to know, and there must be a lot of them in a biography, were spelt 'uv'!

It was the Matthew Bradys my father gave me as a child that have influenced my sense of the past to this day. I have the set. It was the *Review of Reviews* issue of the *Photographic History*. They came, by subscription, I suppose, as thin, large, blue paperbound pamphlets which I could lay open page by page on the floor. The photographs cured me that early of romantic history. I preferred Brady to the colored frontispiece each one carried of some fool's oil on Grant at Lookout Mt or Burnside at Nashville. I could take that as narrative in Joseph Altsheler, *The Rock of Chickamauga*, say. Or in the annual play my father made it a ritual to take me to, even though, each year I ducked behind the back of the seat in front of me when the volley came which cut the hero down. It was year after year, one play, 'The Drummer Boy of Shiloh.'

Once Brady had taught my eyes, I broke through the painted surfaces of war. The dead in Devil's Gulch at Gettysburg, this was something I was not shown at school. Or horses puffed up on a field huge beside the corpses of men or humped in a ditch along some Wilderness road. Or those groups of Brady's, men and women standing with the curiously penetrating eyes Brady's wet plate seemed to fix, at a distance though he was, focussed down on some Virginia 'Station' through a grove of stripped trees. These, too, school did not give me.

Or my father, for that matter. I wonder now what Brady did for him. Maybe, just because I was born here, I had the jump on him. He valued America, as immigrants do, more than the native. I'm not sure it's a good thing. It wasn't, in my father's case, as this trouble he got himself into will show, though for me his fascination with the story of this country was fruitful, as it sometimes is, in the second generation American. There is a sentimentality about the freedoms of this country which none of the bitterness of poverty and abuse will shake in an immigrant. My father had it, at least up to this trouble I write about when the government of these States so failed him he was thrown back on that other rock of the immigrant, his foreign nationality organizations.

〔It took something out of my father's historical soul. From then on he localized his interest to the past of Gloucester and the fishing industry. That, I think, was a gain and, had he lived, it would have given his life and his painting a ground. That was a more usable, economic America than the society of the rights of man which failed him.〕

But he did something else, which was not helpful. To some degree he substituted Sweden for America as a focus for his curiosity, after the 'Americans' failed him in his fight and he had to turn to the Swedish-American societies for aid. They are like mothers anyway, these societies, keeping their children back from the brunt of this country. They aid them but they also fondle them when they are hurt or cut to pieces as they so often are on the steel points of the society.

I think there can be no doubt my father let down and accepted some of this caressing from 1920 on. Nor can I blame him, for he was gravely wounded. I only have this feeling. If he had lived (he was only 52 when he died) I think there was a good chance, given his intelligence and a couple of N.A.L.C. victories he was on the point of winning, that he might have mended. With the help of Gloucester, he might have seen his struggle outside both Sweden and America, as a part of this ambiguous battle all human society is now, for good or evil, engaged in.

It was something of this view that I was trying to give him in his last years, a meagre return for the childhood he gave me. I argued that, if he were to pitch his energies true, he needed to free himself from the narrow area of recrimination into which the enemy had maneuvered him. But I am ahead of my story. Let me say this: I carried one thing home from Plymouth, the broken shaft of an arrow. I found it on the ground behind the stage after the pageant was over.

I better spell the situation out. Postal employees do not have the right to strike. The result is, union organization among carriers and clerks has lagged. On top of that their organizations have tended, because their officers must wheedle and act mostly as lobbyists on Congress, to continue the same men in national office for unhealthy periods of time. The upshot is, the rank and file are about as spiritless a group of workers as you can imagine and their officers have more in common with the Post Office officials than with the men they represent.

This was hardly a condition a fighter like my father could abide. I can't say where he first acquired his sense of workingmen's rights. I think it was more a matter of his bones than training. He had gone to work at fourteen to aid his mother in the support of himself and two sisters. He had a milk route.

He was one of those men for whom newspapers are education. The few times I saw him with a book in his hands he struck me as most awkward, and he soon fell asleep. (The only exception was a complete one. It was *Handy-Andy*. He read it to me nights while I recovered from a tonsil and adenoid operation. I have never, in anyone else's hands, seen a book do like convulsive things.)

I don't even have the impression that his employment as an iron worker, before he became a letter carrier, contributed to him, in any direct way, as a labor organizer. He stayed with the same firm in which he learned the trade, and it was a family business, and a small shop. My father was, in fact, the leader of a crew of master builders. The work of the firm (it was the Stewart Boiler Works) was principally the raising, all over New England, of those huge factory stacks which replaced brick in the expanding days of industry at the turn of the century. For some reason Calais, Maine (I heard it 'callous') came to be the place where I put him when I imagined him high on a staging setting the final lip to the chimney. To this day I can't quite get over the difficulty I then had to figure out how he got down. I could only imagine the descent as made down through the long hole of the completed chimney, and it gave me then, and gives me now, whatever is the inside out of vertigo. It was an exciting thing, this image of him, as a man of heights, and was, I suppose, as satisfying a way as a son can see his father.

Calais, by the way, got chosen, I'm sure, because it looked and sounded strange enough to be a frontier and fitted the map my mind made of the wanderings of this hero of mine as I had constructed it from the tales I picked up. It was a part of the satisfaction I drew from this employment, that it led my father to all sorts of unknown lands and continents in Rhode Island, Massachusetts, New Hampshire and Maine. Calais was Gades, the farthest outpost. It was from Calais, I think, that he proposed to my mother. There was some important business attached to it. Perhaps it was the Canadian stamps on the postcards he sent to her from the town across the river from Calais.

Whatever organizing he had done in his fourteen years in the Post Office before 1920, it was that blow-off which first made me aware that carrying mail involved my father in other things than going away in the morning and returning at night. I knew that occasionally he would go out in the evenings, to what were called 'meetings.' But so far as I was concerned the day reached a climax when he came home from work as the afternoon fell off. I had a habit of waiting for him at the head of the street. (Later it was to watch for him as we played ball in the field which stretched from our backyard as far as Hill's barn. We used to get him to come and knock flies out to us before we'd let him go upstairs.) He was a gay man and I guess I first knew how gay he was the night he came home with what they then called an ulcerated tooth. When I met him and he walked me down the street without a word or greeting I fell into step beside him as troubled as he. His face was so held and his walk so careful I was completely bewildered. I did not dare to look at him more than once or twice. That night the street was very long. It was the first time, I suppose, that I went along a sidewalk in that blind way which causes time and space to distend. Once we were home I had to go out to get flaxseed poultice but he continued to suffer so, the house that night stayed like the street. It was never his teeth again, but from 1920 on he was more often grim, when I met him, than gay.

What happened was this: the postmaster cancelled his vacation the night before we were to leave. It was a most unusual act, and all that I was ever able to find out confirms the fact they did it because my father was the wheelhorse of the union and they wanted, in this small way, to get back at him.

I don't know that they knew he'd play into their hands as he did. The foreman of carriers, Paddy Hehir (hair, the Irish pronounce it), knew my father, and my mother, well. It could be that he knew, and passed on, how much this trip was in my father's mind. But I think not. Paddy's part was otherwise. I'm inclined to believe the bosses didn't know. I'm inclined to think they just decided to balk my father for no other reason than a vacation gave them a chance.

It was Blocky Sheehan, as they called him, the Superintendent of Mails, whom my father, to the end of his life, blamed for the whole business. And Sheehan could only have known the special point of the trip from Paddy or another carrier. As I say, I doubt it was that plotted.

It was the fact that Sheehan and the Postmaster had first granted him permission that forever after was the stake to which my father was tied. It was the injustice of it, the dirty, underhanded trick, I seem to hear him say. He had made Branch 12 of the N.A.L.C. (National Association of Letter Carriers) strong, for the first time, I believe. That was enough. But he was also in correspondence with the State officers of the union and he had already, if my memory is correct, been active in pushing, through the Branch and the annual convention of the N.A.L.C., such programs as national legislation in favor of thirty year optional retirement, the widows' pension, and other like long-range goals. He was a 'trouble-maker.' He and his pal, Dinny Riordan, who had had legal training nights before he became a carrier, were too active for the bosses, too smart, and they figured this was the time to set my father back.

It did, but not the way they thought. He didn't take it. We went off the next morning as planned.

I knew nothing about the trouble of course and to this day I can remember nothing in my father's behaviour that whole week which gave me any clue that there was anything wrong. He did everything to the hilt, as usual. We missed nothing and I still have a sight of one moment of his face as some costume or float or incident in the parade pleased him and I noticed his sudden pleasure, and the way his hair blew. He had taken his hat off, that flat, stiff straw he wore each summer, the old kind with broad straw woven like fish scales, and it had left a red mark on his forehead near the hair, and I noticed it, and beads of sweat.

We saw the pageant night after night. We went aboard the model of the *Mayflower*. We found the old cemetery pitched up over the town. We went out to Duxbury, to Miles Standish and Priscilla Alden's graves. We visited the Plymouth Cordage Company. At least he did. For it seems to me it was there I met him after my Sunday morning venture which became one of those standing jokes in the family.

My mother was a Catholic and I was raised one. The problem was, in Plymouth, where I'd go to mass. Somewhere around the Cordage Co. we found a church my father and I decided must be Catholic. It had the right cross on it, I guess. I went in and he went on, to look over ropes. It wasn't very long when I was out, and so confused to be out so quickly I could not tell him, any more than I could my mother afterwards, that I was sure I had been to a Catholic service. I knew only one thing, that when I had entered handbells were ringing as they are, in the mass, when communion is being prepared. I was sure this at least would satisfy my mother but, on the contrary, it made her only the more upset, for if it were that long after the Gospel that you went in, said she, with a voice that sounded as though she were wringing her hands, you did not hear Mass at all!

For my father the irony of that week must have been that the family we stayed with was that of the Postmaster of North Plymouth! It was one of those gentle houses the New Englanders of the 17th century built and the pleasure of it, of the trees at Duxbury and the sea at Plymouth meant more to me (at least I am stained more with the traces) than the excitements we had come to Plymouth to enjoy. The Postmaster was a Mr. Brown. My father had met him at some convention and it is a measure of how much my father's heart was set on this trip that he had arranged our room with Mr. Brown ahead of time.

It was not like him. I take that from him. He much preferred to set off, recklessly sure that things would work out in their courses. (It was that way the only time we were in New York together. He ended up sharing my hotel room. And forgot his straight edge razor when we left in the morning and only remembered it when we were home. Which worried him, for it was his pride, and he honed it stroke after stroke, wiping the lather off on pieces of toilet paper. He wasn't sure he'd get it back, for we'd left the registration single, to save money, when he had failed to find a room for himself and had come to bunk with me.)

The week passed, and what happened when we returned, so sharply changed life in my home that that week came to mean the end of my childhood. Up to then there had been a cocoon of peace and ease around my nerves. It was so pure it was amniotic, and has left me, it has been my thought, those several years retarded. They multiplied security, my mother and my father were so balanced, and when the change came it tore a fabric so delicate it just blew away.

It is also my thought that, because it was my father who was struck, intensified the role he played for me before and after. He had an added dimension because he was the single image of life, I had lived so long in the sleep of the mother.

They busted him, for insubordination and profanity. It seems he had called Paddy Hehir a son of a bitch when Paddy told him his vacation had been revoked. On top of that, of course, he had done the undoable, when he had up and gone without permission. That was insubordination to duty, to the Postmaster, to the President, to God. There was only one larger crime, to rob the mails.

They had my father, and they didn't let go. The postal system has resemblances to the Army. There is, for example, a demerit system. The offences are graduated and, in their degree, a man's pay is docked. They gave my father the maximum, and our scale of living, poor as it was, went down.

But they didn't stop there. They did the one thing which in those days would cut a veteran letter carrier to the heart. They took my father off his route. Men worked for years to get the routes they wanted. The routes would open as older men retired and the carriers bid for them, by seniority, in turn. Each man had his sense of the kind of route and what part of the city he liked best and this process of selection tended to make both the carrier and the people he served congenial.

For years my father had had the route he wanted. It stretched along the lake which bounds the city on the east. Originally the route ran on both sides of the lake south from the bridge which carried the road to Boston. The bridge alone, and the other wooded side (where nothing much was but the city's amusement park and some summer camps) were enough to make the route what my father would like. Just to cross the bridge a winter morning and a winter afternoon, or to be a part of the boating around it in the summer and the fall, gave his work day a freedom he could never have known in any other route in the city. The whole route had this quality. On the city side it was a series of streets, 'avenues' most of them were called, running parallel to the lake, each a little higher up the gradual slope from it, on which people of small means had built mostly one and a half story homes around the turn of the century. They had left room between themselves and their neighbors and the route was a walker, appropriate to a man with my father's legs and drive. Dogs, for example, ran free and, for some strange reason, attached themselves to him in troupes. (They usually dislike carriers, for the straps they carry, and the way the bag swings when it is unslung from the shoulder. Or so I found when I was a carrier later. They'd come through a screen door to get me in the leg.) My father had so many stories about them that I remember their names and the differences of their natures better than I do most of the people who owned them. He had his favorites for years, who went the whole route with him and who became as well known as he was, along the way. He'd set them off against each other yet see that the butchers in the stores at the corners had meat for them. When one Airedale, Cuppy, was killed by the trolley which ran to the lake down a freeway which cut through the backyards of the settlement, my father was disconsolate for days. There is a picture of him, in a new uniform, with Cuppy pawing him to the shoulders like some mythic lion.

And then there was the life directly on the lake to give the route a fillip a residential area never has. There was the Lincoln Park Theatre on this side of the bridge, to which I was taken on passes in the summer evenings down the freeway in the open cars. And the Chinese who had a wheel concession near the theatre on the Boston road, who each year gave my father, for my mother, some new set of china. (They came packed in a fine straw which interested me.) And the boathouses directly on the lake. Randall's was my father's favorite, or, rather, he was a favorite of the Randalls. Sundays, when the ice was gone, he would take me to Randall's and we would go out together on the lake after a lot of talk between him and the Randall boys during which time I gawked at the racing shells and the canoes set on racks up to the ceiling. And, towards the end of the route south, where the settlement ran off into the woods (in which the city had placed the little herd of what looked to me like moth-eaten buffaloes), was the ice house. My father got me a job there one Christmas vacation when I was in high school and it should have made a man of me. I cut ice with the men from 6 in the morning until 6 at night, and the only thing I can say for the day was, that I waited in terror, for my father's appearance, in the middle of the morning and the afternoon, when he was sure to hail me from the shore and make fun to the men of the way I poled the cakes through the channel into the elevator incline which took the ice up three flights to the house for storing.

Of the people, Martin and Minnie Hester seem to have been the oldest, most continuous friends my father had. I remember the upset when Mr. Hester died. I think he was a carpenter, though I may have this confused with Martin and Nora Reidy. She was my godmother, and Martin was a carpenter in the city school system. Nora marked my birthdays. She always gave me gloves, and was the only one outside the family who remembered my birthday. It fell two days after Christmas. But Martin studded my school days. It was unexpected and delightful to have him turn up at my grammar school. Later, when I was in high school and worked as the cashier at the lunch counter, I saw a lot of him. He used to come over and eat his lunch with me as I sold the tickets. Whenever the Hesters were mentioned it was the life of the Reidys, which I knew intimately (they were brother and sister, both unmarried), that rose up in my mind. I still have to work it out to realize that the Hesters were not a bachelor and an old maid. They remembered my father every Christmas and when he was off the route were most solicitous, though I don't think they played any part in organizing the protest of the people of the route against the Post Office officials. They were too shy.

That was the doing of men like Mr. Lawrence. He had a print shop, and I may remember him more, because he also invented a solution to soften typewriter rollers, and there were a few Saturdays, very few, when I, at my father's urging, made the rounds of the factories in our neighborhood trying to sell the stuff to secretaries and office managers. It was as dreadful to me as another attempt, to sell Mr. Lawrence's letter paper, with the name done to order. (The only time door to door selling interested me was Christmas cards, for the Waltham Company, and that took no selling, and gave me a huge profit, 50¢ on a dollar box.) But Mr. Lawrence stands in my mind as one of the leaders who called the several meetings at the Lake, as we called the route, to take action to get my father back.

I recall the Biancis, mostly for the huge Italian dinner, my first spaghetti and meatballs, that we and the Foleys were invited to. I have the feeling they were on Pat Foley's route, which joined my father's on the city side.

Most of the other names are gone. There were the Siskins, who had the meat market, and who spoiled my father's dogs. But the others, though remnants of my father's talk about them swim in my mind, have lost their faces and their names. There was an Irish girl who kept house for the priests, and it was one of my father's favorite diversions to plague her with his skepticisms about religion when he knew that one of the curates was listening in the next room. Once, with great care, he decorated and wrapped a brick as a fool's present for her, in lieu of what object she wanted I can't say. He was given to wrapping and boxing minute presents in huge boxes which he had the parcel post carrier deliver with extra fanfare. This seems to have been a part of the give and take of the route. He came home once with a box of fool's candy, soft ones of pepper, nougats of tobacco, thin ones of cardboard. He had been taken in and tried them on us.

I imagine the ones I have remembered are those with whom I had something to do. The vast majority I never saw, even though on one grand occasion I went the route with my father. I must have been about twelve. I don't know what the occasion was, but I do recall the place that impressed me most. It was the State Insane Hospital. It occupied the whole of the hill to the lake on the opposite side of the Boston road from the body of my father's route. The buildings, brownstone and like a college, were at the top and the farm ran down the slope behind a fence which seems to me now to have been made of rails, though it probably was of stone. It was along this fence that the inmates sat or walked, and their eyes, clothes, postures and gestures were a world of people I found much more interesting than the rest of us. From that day on, whenever I would go to the Lake of a Sunday or could get my father to talk, it was these men I wanted to see and hear of. They got mixed up in my mind with Brady's people of the Civil War. When I was told that the Reidys' sister Agnes had died in that hospital I could not bring the fact together with the fable the men along the fence stood for. (I even had some of the same difficulty much, much later when Martin Reidy was taken there. It was after my mother had lived with them, the winter following my father's death. I had visited with them at Christmas and though there was a difference in Nora and Martin [Nora had always made me nervous ever since the hate she showed in arguments with my father over the Germans during the first world war] I attributed it to age. The house still smelled of Martin's good tobacco and was as remarkably neat as Nora had always kept it. No one was prepared for the crisis when it came. One night Nora waked to find Martin going around the house with an axe, looking under all the beds and accusing her of intimate relations with their nephew who lived upstairs.) Some of the nuts, as they were called, were free to leave the grounds and used to walk my father's route with him. One carved things as presents for him. My father gave them smokes and clothes.

That route was my father's parish, village to which he was crier and walking mayor. He was more intimate to the community, and the lives of all the people, than anyone else could be. The people showed it, the way they fought for him, when the crisis came.

Some of it was himself but part the fact he was 'the postman.' Mail, over any length of time, will tell secrets a neighbor could not guess. Nor do I mean the reading of postcards or the 'lamping' of letters. Nor what a man hears over coffee. Or that a man's mail does not always come to his house, or a woman's either. It lies more in the manner in which people look for, ask for, receive their mail. And talk about it.

A letter, expected or surprise, is a lance, and the vizor slips, and I talk to this person to get it back into place, for I know him every day and yet I do not know him so well a confidence will lead me anywhere. I am aware I am vulnerable and I will regret a little some of the things I am saying, but... the uniform makes Mr. Olson anonymous enough.

This was most true in the days before Burleson, Wilson's Postmaster General, took the craft and country quality out of the service. The loss was the loss common to most labor since. This better be understood as not nostalgia. I was a letter carrier myself later and do not hark back. We have got so used to change that we are unwilling to believe that suddenly some change may be so total as to destroy. The path does die, and there are times when, to find his way back, man has to pick up, fiercely and without any easy emotion, traces of the way. What happened to work during the first world war is a trace.

Carrying mail never did require great skill any more than most of the broad-gauged jobs which make society run. You have heard all either of us wants to hear of the carrier the Man of Weather – sleet snow night rain: excelsior. What is not mentioned are hernia rheumatism flatfeet death (insurance company average) 52. The hazards. I can add, of Charles Olson Sr., (1) a fall down a flight of 30 stone steps & like incidents in the line of duty, (2) the morning he was brought home, before I had left for school, to my mother's and my surprise – a trolley car had split a switch and spread him out full six foot three on the pavement at Front and Pleasant Streets. This kind of weather lasts.

What can be lost is the weather of a man. What gave the carrier dignity, the sense of accomplishment, what made his day of use to the people he served as well as to himself was the illusion that how he did it was of value.

Here is the connection between Burleson and what the bosses did to my father. My father did not want union power. He never held or sought top office. He served some terms as secretary, but not to control from that powerful post. To get the work done. For several years I did his typing and can say. What he was after, what all the legislation he pushed was directed against, was the speed-up. I used to get pretty bored with figures on the occupational diseases of letter carriers, calculations on the differentials of the volume of mail over a month, statistics on the condition of the widows of carriers, numbers of children per family etc., but it is clear that he saw what the fight was.

I'm sure the bosses were too knowing to think he could take the union over. He did not have that will and if he had they knew how to buy such men off. In some awkward way, with no scheme or large sense of what was involved, out of the needs of his own personality, his assurance that the satisfaction of a job lay in the perfection of the doing of it, the pounding of a rivet, the use of pumice after sandpaper to make a surface ready for a stain, the fixative to set a crayon sketch for O. Victor Humann at the Museum, led my father to fight for quality against efficiency in the postal service. That was, and is, the battle-line.

He was the resistance of a man, my father, the cry of the individual that he be allowed the time and the conditions to do his work, as they used to say, right. And that's why the bosses went after him. They attacked him because he wanted to do his work too well. He was unhealthy to have around. The speed-up might irk the other men but they would be unprepared, as most men are, from confusion and the hundred costs the family is heir to, to do anything. They would go along, even though it meant they'd wither and go dead. My father's threat to the bosses was not so much his activity as himself. He was an image to the other men of what they had

II. PARENTS

been, a trace to the younger men of what work was. He had to be harassed.

Today he'd be fired. Or not hired in the first place. Or, if a company had to show a payroll for a contract, be the first laid off. Ground has been lost. But a good worker still knows, and can tell you, what my father knew. He just happened to be one of the first, and it was clearer earlier in the postal service than in heavy industry. He was at the switch point when the turn came. He was no enemy. He was opposition. He was fighting for pride in work which is personality. It is that simple. We have forgotten what men crave. We think that all workers want is pay. But that's all they are left with, where production, and that rot of modern work, efficiency, rule. Give workers only that and they'll featherbed you back. If you take away pride you'll have to give prizes. And why not? Corner men and they are good animals: they know how to resist.

Behind his bosses were the postal inspectors. Behind them Burleson. Behind Burleson the huge forfeit of pro-duction. It is old George Harris' proposition: bishops eats elders, elders eats common peopil, they eats sich cattil as me, I eats possums, possums eats chickins, chickins swallers wums, an' wums is content to eat dus, an' dus is the aind uv hit all.

Only hit ain't. The dus is the kulchur daid on the groun'. For example. My father was old fashion. He had notions having to do with courtesy, modesty, care, proportion, respect. He had them confused with his work. A letter say. He was scrupulous about a letter. He had the idea it was somehow important just because it was made up of words (he had the notion that words have value, as signs of meaning and feeling) and because it was a communication between two persons (the idea of a person seems to have meant something to him). Thus he took himself seriously as the last, and only directly personal agent, of several hired by a stamp to see that a letter reached the person to whom it was addressed or, rather (as I am sure he, with his notions, would have put it) for whom it was meant.

As a part of such motion he took himself to be responsible. (He was. I have known him, of an evening after work, to be as concerned as to whether a party on his route had got a letter they had been expecting which he had had to leave in their box because they were not at home, as another man might be concerned about well, say, the safe, or whether he had locked the office door.) A good carrier did not jam cards. He did not leave insured parcels carelessly. He stopped to ring and wait to get the mail inside when the weather was bad. He held mail for people when they were away, or forwarded for them, without delay. The niceties.

And the accommodations: bring stamps to people, or take their letters and buy the stamps for them. Or small packages or magazines, where they did not know the weight. Even a laundry, once in a while.

And registered mail: to let people know they could send money directly by you instead of going up town to the post office to do it, as most people think they have to. The finish on the work. (It was my father who first told me the answer of the cabinet maker to the looker-on who was making fun of the care the c.m. was giving to the under side of a table. 'Why bother your self. No one will ever, in this world, notice that.' Drawls the c.m., switching his chaw, 'I notice it.'

All of which courtesies take   took   time.
Enter: the route inspector.
From 1920 on my father was never left long at peace on his route without there was, suddenly, any day, a route inspector on his back. As he would leave the Post Office for his route there would be some guy, known or unknown, with his sheet of paper and his yellow look (the look of the checker in any business) who would go the route with him that day to 'clock him,' to count the pieces and the time. It was the way the bosses hounded a man, in Post Office talk.

They had another trick. When a man went on vacation they'd assign a special substitute to carry the route, a man whom the regulars called a route-killer, some bird who wanted to stand in with the foreman of carriers to get extra work and who was ready, for that reason, or from plain fear, to run around the route and get in under the regular's time. I had one once myself. He managed a ball club. A route was something he got rid of as soon as he could (though he was paid, as I was, by the hour) in order to have time to chew the fat with his players at noon or get the bases out to the field at night. He came in one day two hours under my time! That finished me on that route. They transferred me to a truck!

But I was a kid, and didn't care. With my father it was different. It was his life work. He got so he was grim and dangerous over this business. If he'd have been a machinist, they had turned him into such a bitter, revengeful man, he would have gone beyond the slow-down. He would have turned saboteur, and wrecked machinery. As it was he went illegal. He worked out a trick to beat them. It was to increase the mail the day they inspected him. He did it in one of two ways. On at least one occasion (at the height of his trouble, I'd say, from the way I remember it) when he was tipped off ahead of time that he was going to get it, he mailed first class stuff himself the night before, in several different handwritings to people on the route. Another time, it seems to me, he called my mother during the morning and had her drop some similar letters he had ready in order to fatten the afternoon delivery on his route. But the other device was simpler. It rested on the increase of advertising circulars in the 20s and 30s. It was mostly third class mail, and carriers were not obliged to deliver it the day it came in, if such a piece meant adding distance to the route. But my father went much further in his determination to beat the inspection system. He would cull out these circulars until he had a selected bunch of them well distributed around his route. These he would keep hidden in his locker or perhaps it was behind his sorting case at the post office. When an inspector was due out with him he would sort these pieces in with the day's mail. It took up the slack. (I should make clear that it was the custom, when the higher-ups were after a man, to send an inspector out at that time of the month or the week when the mail is lightest. Monday is such a day. The first of the month is the heaviest.)

It was a mischievous business, and my father lived with it nervously. (He had a bad time of it the day he discovered new cases had arrived and there had been some shifting of the old ones during the morning when he was out on the route.) My impression is, this stupid bundle of mail was on his mind all the years up to his death. There it sat, the only illegal thing he'd ever done, the one thing, and the only thing, if they found it, which would give them the goods they wished they had on him. His record was clean, clean as a whistle is the way he would have put it, if he was of a mind to talk about himself. Yet here he himself ran the risk of giving them the very thing they wanted. And why? Merely to beat them at a game which he took as an insult to his amour propre.

This is what I meant by his stubbornness. He wanted his route the way it had been before the speed-up. He wanted his route the way he had built it, with time left in for the courtesies, the niceties, and a coffee now and then. But there was a side to this desire, after his trouble, which has to be put this way: he wanted it the way it had been because the bosses wanted it different. The fact of the matter is he wanted to overprove his point with some idea that in so doing he made more apparent the dirtiness of their attack on him. Which, of course, was not so. He could easily have turned the point of any of their tricks by merely continuing as he had been. He had a long route and no one could have squeezed it much. The proof is, that when they finally decided he had suffered enough, after the Plymouth deal, they put him back on the route pretty much, as far as I can remember, as he had been beforehand. In other words the hounding took. The only thing it didn't do was break his will. He didn't give in. He only died.

It took fourteen years. The demerits came first. Then the removal from the route. At that point they pulled another military move. They required him to tear off the three red stars from his sleeve, for the fifteen years he had served. For they had a final ignominy. I suppose it is possible they thought they could drive him out of the service altogether. Anyhow they assigned him to the lowest job there is, the job the greenest sub carrier gets, the night collection.

I don't remember how long they kept him on it. It may have been a year. I'm not sure, now that I am further down into the past, if I am right they took him off his route immediately on our return from Plymouth. I'm not sure they didn't inspect the life out of him first, having docked his pay, and that it wasn't on one of these inspections that he called Paddy Hehir or maybe it was Blocky Sheehan a son of a bitch. In any case the night collection was the final punishment.

One thing stands out, a picture that Dinny Riordan gave me the day my father died. It was a sudden death, cerebral hemorrhage, the first shock on a Thursday paralyzing the right side, the second one, Saturday morning, getting the heart. What Dinny revealed to me was that in 1920, apparently not long after the start of the trouble, he and my father were on a streetcar going to their routes. (Dinny's was the next above the route adjoining my father's.) Suddenly as they were sitting there in the long seat at the back of the car Dinny became aware that my father was not listening to him, was in fact leaning slightly against him and looking off with a fixed look out the windows across the aisle. He thought my father was joking, or something, and gave him a shove. It was the way my father came out of it that made Dinny first aware that something was wrong. He said nothing, and nothing more was mentioned about it. But the doctors told me, when I checked with them, that it was the premonitory shock. The trouble had brought it on. Shortly after, in going over my father's papers, I discovered that it was the very year, 1920, that had begun the annual checkups with the doctor which were dramatized for me by the urine bottle.

The nights must have been dirt in my father's mouth, the city's main streets, letters in lumps, people to ask why he was there. Or to say, what's this we see in the papers. For he fought back from the start. The senator was David I. Walsh. He tried to reach him. The congressman was Pehr Holmes, a Swede. He saw him. Promises, letters, meetings, articles. The NALC. The branch of UNIPOX (Un. PO Clerks). I don't figure, now, that it was long before he was back on the route. But that, alas, was not the end of the struggle. It never ended for him. Somehow he had to pay them back, Hehir, Sheehan, and the Postmaster, Healy. He increased his work in the Branch. He widened out to the national officers. He joined the Carl the 15th Lodge, the Swedish American Federation. The paper *Svea* had helped in the struggle. He became a friend of Karl Fredin the editor. His Swedish began to come back. He began to get me to speak to their festivals. He became more and more involved. More evenings went out from his drawing, his piano playing. The one thing he did not lessen was Gloucester.

Gloucester became the one offset. He would come each weekend, arranging rides for himself if he could, or hopping the train. Only in Gloucester was he free from revenge. And it was from Gloucester that he left the last time I saw him whole. He was to go the next weekend to the National Convention of the Carriers at Cleveland. It was to be a big business, for he and his cronies around the country (he had built up a terrific correspondence) were hoping they could turn out the old officers and put in Ferd Douglas of Brooklyn. It was one of the payoffs my father intended, for the officers of the NALC had failed him, he thought, in his fight. He was out to get them. It was to be a big thing, and when he was leaving he waked me to ask if I would let him take my suitcase which was bigger and newer than his. I had a use for it that coming weekend which seemed important to me, and I refused. He went away sore, and the curious thing is, that though my mother and I drove the hundred miles to the hospital the moment we heard he was sick and though I was with him much of the time until he died, I do not remember that he ever addressed me or seemed to notice that I was there. He pinched my mother's nose and said something unintelligible from the twist of his mouth but it is only now that I realize at no time did he admit a notice of me. Or do I exaggerate and punish myself anew for the guilt of my refusal of the suitcase. I do not know. What I do know is that the house, when we got back to it, showed that all that week he must have stayed up night after night preparing the papers and resolutions that were to be used at the Convention. That was 1934. Plymouth was all those years back, yet here he was locked in the struggle which issued from it. He had won the fight, and lost it, god help us all.

As the Dead Prey Upon Us

'To write a dream which shall resemble the real course of a dream, with all its inconsistency, its strange transformations, which are all taken as a matter of course, its eccentricities and aimlessness – with nevertheless a leading idea running through the whole' – Olson, whether knowingly or not, fulfils this recipe of Ralph Waldo Emerson's in 'As the Dead Prey Upon Us', the original title of which was 'To Alleviate the Dream'. In another typescript it was 'The Mother Poem', presumably in recognition of the 'leading idea running through the whole'. Written five years after his mother's death, the poem is given a continuum of elegaic commentary in which Olson's voice rises toward the end into a fierceness that takes the Buddhist 'five hindrances' (supposedly holding us to retrograde things, perhaps like a mother's arms) and inverts them scornfully to opportunities.

As the dead prey upon us,
they are the dead in ourselves,
awake, my sleeping ones, I cry out to you,
disentangle the nets of being!

I pushed my car, it had been sitting so long unused.
I thought the tires looked as though they only needed air.
But suddenly the huge underbody was above me, and the rear tires
were masses of rubber and thread variously clinging together

as were the dead souls in the living room, gathered
about my mother, some of them taking care to pass
beneath the beam of the movie projector, some record
playing on the victrola, and all of them
desperate with the tawdriness of their life in hell

I turned to the young man on my right and asked, 'How is it,
there?' And he begged me protestingly don't ask, we are poor
poor. And the whole room was suddenly posters and presentations
of brake linings and other automotive accessories, cardboard
displays, the dead roaming from one to another
as bored back in life as they are in hell, poor and doomed
to mere equipments

II. PARENTS

        my mother, as alive as ever she was, asleep
when I entered the house as I often found her in a rocker
under the lamp, and awaking, as I came up to her, as she ever had

I found out she returns to the house once a week, and with her
the throng of the unknown young who center on her as much in death
as other like suited and dressed people did in life

O the dead!

        and the Indian woman and I
        enabled the blue deer
        to walk

        and the blue deer talked,
        in the next room,
        a Negro talk

        it was like walking a jackass,
        and its talk
        was the pressing gabber of gammers
        of old women

        and we helped walk it around the room
        because it was seeking socks
        or shoes for its hooves
        now that it was acquiring

        human possibilities

In the five hindrances men and angels
stay caught in the net, in the immense nets
which spread out across each plane of being, the multiple nets
which hamper at each step of the ladders as the angels
and the demons
and men
go up and down

        Walk the jackass
        Hear the victrola
        Let the automobile

     be tucked into a corner of the white fence
     when it is a white chair. Purity

is only an instant of being, the trammels
recur

In the five hindrances, perfection
is hidden

      I shall get
      to the place
      10 minutes late.

      It will be 20 minutes
      of 9. And I don't know,

     without the car,

     how I shall get there

O peace, my mother, I do not know
how differently I could have done
what I did or did not do.

      That you are back each week
      that you fall asleep
      with your face to the right

      that you are as present there
      when I come in as you were
      when you were alive

      that you are as solid, and your flesh
      is as I knew it, that you have the company
      I am used to your having

      but o, that you all find it
      such a cheapness!

o peace, mother, for the mammothness
of the comings and goings

II. PARENTS

of the ladders of life

The nets we are entangled in. Awake,
my soul, let the power into the last wrinkle
of being, let none of the threads and rubber of the tires
be left upon the earth. Let even your mother
go. Let there be only paradise

The desperateness is, that the instant
which is also paradise (paradise
is happiness) dissolves
into the next instant, and power
flows to meet the next occurrence

               Is it any wonder
               my mother comes back?
               Do not that throng
               rightly seek the room
               where they might expect
               happiness? They did not complain
               of life, they obviously wanted
               the movie, each other, merely to pass
               among each other there,
where the real is, even to the display cards,
to be out of hell

          The poverty
          of hell

O souls, in life and in death,
awake, even as you sleep, even in sleep
know what wind
even under the crankcase of the ugly automobile
lifts it away, clears the sodden weights of goods,
equipment, entertainment, the foods the Indian woman,
the filthy blue deer, the 4 by 3 foot 'Viewbook,'
the heaviness of the old house, the stuffed inner room
lifts the sodden nets

               and they disappear as ghosts do,
               as spider webs, nothing

before the hand of man

The vent! You must have the vent,
or you shall die. Which means
never to die, the ghastliness

of going, and forever
coming back, returning
to the instants which were not lived

O mother, this I could not have done,
I could not have lived what you didn't,
I am myself netted in my own being

I want to die. I want to make that instant, too,
perfect

O my soul, slip
the cog

II

The death in life (death itself)
is endless, eternity
is the false cause

The knot is other wise, each topological corner
presents itself, and no sword
cuts it, each knot is itself its fire

each knot of which the net is made
is for the hands to untake
the knot's making. And touch alone
can turn the knot into its own flame

              (o mother, if you had once touched me

            o mother, if I had once touched you)

The car did not burn. Its underside

was not presented to me
a grotesque corpse. The old man

merely removed it as I looked up at it,
and put it in a corner of the picket fence
like was it my mother's white dog?

or a child's chair

                The woman,
                playing on the grass,
                with her son (the woman next door)

                was angry with me whatever it was
                slipped across the playpen or whatever
                she had out there on the grass

                And I was quite flip in reply
                that anyone who used plastic
                had to expect things to skid

                and break, that I couldn't worry
                that her son might have been hurt
                by whatever it was I sent skidding

                down on them.

                It was just then I went into my house
                and to my utter astonishment
                found my mother sitting there
                as she always had sat, as must she always
                forever sit there her head lolling
                into sleep? Awake, awake my mother

                what wind will lift you too
                forever from the tawdriness,
                make you rich as all those souls

                crave   crave   crave

                to be rich?

They are right. We must have
what we want. We cannot afford
not to. We have only one course:

the nets which entangle us are flames

> O souls, burn
> alive, burn now
>
> that you may forever
> have peace, have
>
> what you crave
>
> O souls,
> go into everything,
> let not one knot pass
> through your fingers
>
> let not any they tell you
> you must sleep as the net
> comes through your authentic hands
>
> What passes
> is what is, what shall be, what has
> been, what hell and heaven is
> is earth to be rent, to shoot you
> through the screen of flame which each knot
> hides as all knots are a wall ready
> to be shot open by you
>
>   the nets of being
> are only eternal if you sleep as your hands
> ought to be busy. Method, method
>
> I too call on you to come
> to the aid of all men, to women most
> who know most, to woman to tell
> men to awake. Awake, men,
> awake

I ask my mother
to sleep. I ask her
to stay in the chair.
My chair
is in the corner of the fence.
She sits by the fireplace made of paving stones. The blue deer
need not trouble either of us.

And if she sits in happiness the souls
who trouble her and me
will also rest. The automobile

has been hauled away.

III. Projective Verse

As with any *ars poetica* where the commentary arises from the available body of writing, Olson's 'Projective Verse' (1950) was basically a summary of the kind of poetry he had just found himself able to produce, a style inaugurated by 'The Kingfishers'. The ideas were essentially liberating, as Olson himself felt newly liberated. It is ironic that Olson has probably become more well-known for this bit of theorising than anything else he did. Though 'Projective Verse' was never in any danger of being renounced by Olson, we should note that it was, after all, very early in his writing career.

The Kingfishers

Olson characterised this poem as 'an examination-confrontation of America as such versus predictions of and from the East Wind' (Guide, p. xxvi). Mao Tse-tung really is a figure of the future here, and the kingfishers are Western civilisation in decline from its hopeful beginnings with the E on the stone at Delphi. And what can the individual American do about it? The answer is a cautious positive: one can marshall one's forces to 'hunt among stones'. This is a pivotal turning away from the anomie of The Waste Land. *Olson saw the poem as an 'Anti-Waste Land', and wanted it to be as important for his own time as Eliot's had been for his. As the first poem in Donald Allen's influencial anthology* The New American Poetry 1945-1960 *(New York: Grove Press 1960), it received some such attention through the turbulent decade of the 1960s.*

1
What does not change / is the will to change

He woke, fully clothed, in his bed. He
remembered only one thing, the birds, how
when he came in, he had gone around the rooms
and got them back in their cage, the green one first,
she with the bad leg, and then the blue,
the one they had hoped was a male

Otherwise? Yes, Fernand, who had talked lispingly of Albers & Angkor
                                                                                                   Vat.
He had left the party without a word. How he got up, got into his coat,

I do not know. When I saw him, he was at the door, but it did not matter,
he was already sliding along the wall of the night, losing himself
in some crack of the ruins. That it should have been he who said, 'The
                                                        kingfishers!
who cares
for their feathers
now?'

His last words had been, 'The pool is slime.' Suddenly everyone,
ceasing their talk, sat in a row around him, watched
they did not so much hear, or pay attention, they
wondered, looked at each other, smirked, but listened,
he repeated and repeated, could not go beyond his thought
'The pool   the kingfishers' feathers were wealth   why
did the export stop?'

It was then he left

2
I thought of the E on the stone, and of what Mao said

la lumiere'
         but the kingfisher
de l'aurore'
         but the kingfisher flew west
est devant nous!
         he got the color of his breast
         from the heat of the setting sun!

The features are, the feebleness of the feet   (syndactylism of the
                                                       3rd & 4th digit)
the bill, serrated, sometimes a pronounced beak, the wings
where the color is, short and round, the tail
inconspicuous.

But not these things were the factors. Not the birds.
The legends are
legends. Dead, hung up indoors, the kingfisher
will not indicate a favoring wind,
or avert the thunderbolt. Nor, by its nesting,
still the waters, with the new year, for seven days.

It is true, it does nest with the opening year, but not on the waters.
It nests at the end of a tunnel bored by itself in a bank. There,
six or eight white and translucent eggs are laid, on fishbones
not on bare clay, on bones thrown up in pellets by the birds.

                On these rejectamenta
(as they accumulate they form a cup-shaped structure) the young are born.
And, as they are fed and grow, this nest of excrement and decayed
                                                fish becomes
                    a dripping, fetid mass

Mao concluded:
        nous devons
                nous lever
                        et agir!

3
When the attentions change / the jungle
leaps in
        even the stones are split
                they rive

Or,
enter
that other conqueror we more naturally recognize
he so resembles ourselves

But the E
cut so rudely on that oldest stone
sounded otherwise,
was differently heard

as, in another time, were treasures used:

(and, later, much later, a fine ear thought
a scarlet coat)

        'of green feathers   feet, beaks and eyes
        of gold

III. PROJECTIVE VERSE

'animals likewise,
resembling snails

'a large wheel, gold, with figures of unknown four-foots,
and worked with tufts of leaves, weight
3800 ounces

'last, two birds, of thread and featherwork, the quills
gold, the feet
gold, the two birds perched on two reeds
gold, the reeds arising from two embroidered mounds,
one yellow, the other
white.
        'And from each reed hung
        seven feathered tassels.

In this instance, the priests
(in dark cotton robes, and dirty,
their dishevelled hair matted with blood, and flowing wildly
over their shoulders)
rush in among the people, calling on them
to protect their gods

And all now is war
where so lately there was peace,
and the sweet brotherhood, the use
of tilled fields.

4
Not one death but many,
not accumulation but change, the feed-back proves, the feed-back is
the law
        Into the same river no man steps twice
        When fire dies air dies
        No one remains, nor is, one

Around an appearance, one common model, we grow up
many. Else how is it,
if we remain the same,
we take pleasure now
in what we did not take pleasure before? love

contrary objects? admire and/or find fault? use
other words, feel other passions, have
nor figure, appearance, disposition, tissue
the same?
     To be in different states without a change
     is not a possibility

We can be precise. The factors are
in the animal and/or the machine the factors are
communication and/or control, both involve
the message. And what is the message? The message is
a discrete or continuous sequence of measurable events distributed in time

is the birth of air, is
the birth of water, is
a state between
the origin and
the end, between
birth and the beginning of
another fetid nest

is change, presents
no more than itself

And the too strong grasping of it,
when it is pressed together and condensed,
loses it

This very thing you are

                      II

     They buried their dead in a sitting posture
     serpent   cane   razor   ray of the sun

     And she sprinkled water on the head of the child, crying
     'Cioa-coatl! Cioa-coatl!'
     with her face to the west

     Where the bones are found, in each personal heap
     with what each enjoyed, there is always
     the Mongolian louse

The light is in the east. Yes. And we must rise, act. Yet
in the west, despite the apparent darkness (the whiteness
which covers all), if you look, if you can bear, if you can, long enough

        as long as it was necessary for him, my guide
        to look into the yellow of that longest-lasting rose

so you must, and, in that whiteness, into that face, with what candor, look

and, considering the dryness of the place
    the long absence of an adequate race

        (of the two who first came, each a conquistator, one
                            healed, the other
        tore the eastern idols down, toppled
        the temple walls, which, says the excuser
        were black from human gore)

hear
hear, where the dry blood talks
    where the old appetite walks

                la piu saporita et migliore
                che si posse truovar al mondo

where it hides, look
in the eye how it runs
in the flesh / chalk

        but under these petals
        in the emptiness
        regard the light, contemplate
        the flower

whence it arose

        with what violence benevolence is bought
        what cost in gesture justice brings
        what wrongs domestic rights involve
        what stalks
        this silence

what pudor pejorocracy affronts
how awe, night-rest and neighborhood can rot
what breeds where dirtiness is law
what crawls
below

III

I am no Greek, hath not th'advantage.
And of course, no Roman:
he can take no risk that matters,
the risk of beauty least of all.

But I have my kin, if for no other reason than
(as he said, next of kin) I commit myself, and,
given my freedom, I'd be a cad
if I didn't. Which is most true.

It works out this way, despite the disadvantage.
I offer, in explanation, a quote:
si j'ai du goût, ce n'est guères
que pour la terre et les pierres.

Despite the discrepancy (an ocean   courage   age)
this is also true: if I have any taste
it is only because I have interested myself
in what was slain in the sun

    I pose you your question:

shall you uncover honey / where maggots are?

    I hunt among stones

Projective Verse

Olson, when asked, said he knew about projective geometry; but one does not have to go that far afield when the main clue to the title is in the first paragraph of the essay and reiterated throughout: the breath itself. The verse line comes up from the heart, but also from the diaphragm. It is breathed out on to the page, being projected to the reader as though to an audience in a theatre. The length of each line is the 'projectile' arc, is what the content provides 'percussive' energy for in the instant that the poet's 'prospective' eye perceives it. The crucial role of the content is what Olson coined the word 'objectism' for, in an attempt to cut down to proper size self-centred lyric humanism.

That Olson accomplished the ars poetica *for his time that he had hoped to do received confirmation when William Carlos Williams 'leaped out of bed' on 16 December 1950 to write to Olson for permission to use the essay verbatim in his* Autobiography *because he had suddenly realised that it was 'the keystone, the most admirable piece of thinking about the poem that I recently, perhaps ever, encountered' (*Muthologos *2.190).*

PROJECTIVE   VERSE

       (projectile   (percussive   (prospective

vs.

THE NON-PROJECTIVE

(or what a French critic calls 'closed' verse, that verse which print bred and which is pretty much what we have had, in English & American, and have still got, despite the work of Pound & Williams:

it led Keats, already a hundred years ago, to see it (Wordsworth's, Milton's) in the light of 'the Egotistical Sublime'; and it persists, at this latter day, as what you might call the private-soul-at-any-public-wall)

Verse now, 1950, if it is to go ahead, if it is to be of *essential* use, must, I take it, catch up and put into itself certain laws and possibilities of the breath, of the breathing of the man who writes as well as of his listenings. (The revolution of the ear, 1910, the trochee's heave, asks it of the younger poets.)

I want to do two things: first, try to show what projective or OPEN verse is, what it involves, in its act of composition, how, in distinction from the non-projective, it is accomplished; and II, suggest a few ideas about what stance toward reality brings such verse into being, what that stance does, both to the poet and to his reader. (The stance involves, for example, a change beyond, and larger than, the technical, and may, the way things look, lead to new poetics and to new concepts from which some sort of drama, say, or of epic, perhaps, may emerge.)

I

First, some simplicities that a man learns, if he works in OPEN, or what can also be called COMPOSITION BY FIELD, as opposed to inherited line, stanza, over-all form, what is the 'old' base of the non-projective.

(1) the *kinetics* of the thing. A poem is energy transferred from where the poet got it (he will have some several causations), by way of the poem itself to, all the way over to, the reader. Okay. Then the poem itself must, at all points, be a high energy-construct and, at all points, an energy-discharge. So: how is the poet to accomplish same energy, how is he, what is the process by which a poet gets in, at all points energy at least the equivalent of the energy which propelled him in the first place, yet an energy which is peculiar to verse alone and which will be, obviously, also different from the energy which the reader, because he is a third term, will take away?

This is the problem which any poet who departs from closed form is specially confronted by. And it involves a whole series of new recognitions. From the moment he ventures into FIELD COMPOSITION – puts himself in the open – he can go by no track other than the one the poem under hand declares, for itself. Thus he has to behave, and be, instant by instant, aware of some several forces just now beginning to be examined. (It is much more, for example, this push, than simply such a one as Pound put, so wisely, to get us started: 'the musical phrase', go by it, boys, rather than by, the metronome.)

(2) is the *principle*, the law which presides conspicuously over such composition, and, when obeyed, is the reason why a projective poem can come into being. It is this: FORM IS NEVER MORE THAN AN EXTENSION OF CONTENT. (Or so it got phrased by one, R. Creeley, and it makes absolute sense to me, with this possible corollary, that

right form, in any given poem, is the only and exclusively possible extension of content under hand.) There it is, brothers, sitting there, for USE.

Now (3) the *process* of the thing, how the principle can be made so to shape the energies that the form is accomplished. And I think it can be boiled down to one statement (first pounded into my head by Edward Dahlberg): ONE PERCEPTION MUST IMMEDIATELY AND DIRECTLY LEAD TO A FURTHER PERCEPTION. It means exactly what it says, is a matter of, at *all* points (even, I should say, of our management of daily reality as of the daily work) get on with it, keep moving, keep in, speed, the nerves, their speed, the perceptions, theirs, the acts, the split second acts, the whole business, keep it moving as fast as you can, citizen. And if you also set up as a poet, USE USE USE the process at all points, in any given poem always, always one perception must must must MOVE, INSTANTER, ON ANOTHER!

So there we are, fast, there's the dogma. And its excuse, its usableness, in practice. Which gets us, it ought to get us, inside the machinery, now, 1950, of how projective verse is made.

If I hammer, if I recall in, and keep calling in, the breath, the breathing as distinguished from the hearing, it is for cause, it is to insist upon a part that breath plays in verse which has not (due, I think, to the smothering of the power of the line by too set a concept of foot) has not been sufficiently observed or practiced, but which has to be if verse is to advance to its proper force and place in the day, now, and ahead. I take it that PROJECTIVE VERSE teaches, is, this lesson, that that verse will only do in which a poet manages to register both the acquisitions of his ear *and* the pressures of his breath.

Let's start from the smallest particle of all, the syllable. It is the king and pin of versification, what rules and holds together the lines, the larger forms, of a poem. I would suggest that verse here and in England dropped this secret from the late Elizabethans to Ezra Pound, lost it, in the sweetness of meter and rime, in a honey-head. (The syllable is one way to distinguish the original success of blank verse, and its falling off, with Milton.)

It is by their syllables that words juxtapose in beauty, by these particles of sound as clearly as by the sense of the words which they compose. In any given instance, because there is a choice of words, the choice, if a man is in there, will be, spontaneously, the obedience of his ear to the syllables. The fineness, and the practice, lie here, at the minimum and source of speech.

> O western wynd, when wilt thou blow
> And the small rain down shall rain
> O Christ that my love were in my arms
> And I in my bed again

It would do no harm, as an act of correction to both prose and verse as now written, if both rime and meter, and, in the quantity words, both sense and sound, were less in the forefront of the mind than the syllable, if the syllable, that fine creature, were more allowed to lead the harmony on. With this warning, to those who would try: to step back here to this place of the elements and minims of language, is to engage speech where it is least careless – and least logical. Listening for the syllables must be so constant and so scrupulous, the exaction must be so complete, that the assurance of the ear is purchased at the highest – 40 hour a day – price. For from the root out, from all over the place, the syllable comes, the figures of, the dance:

> 'Is' comes from the Aryan root, *as*, to breathe.
> The English 'not' equals the Sanscrit *na*, which
> may come from the root *na*, to be lost, to perish.
> 'Be' is from *bhu*, to grow.

I say the syllable, king, and that it is spontaneous, this way: the ear, the ear which has collected, which has listened, the ear, which is so close to the mind that it is the mind's, that it has the mind's speed...

it is close, another way: the mind is brother to this sister and is, because it is so close, is the drying force, the incest, the sharpener...

it is from the union of the mind and the ear that the syllable is born.

But the syllable is only the first child of the incest of verse (always, that Egyptian thing, it produces twins!). The other child is the LINE. And together, these two, the syllable *and* the line, they make a poem, they make that thing, the – what shall we call it, the Boss of all, the 'Single Intelligence'. And the line comes (I swear it) from the breath, from the breathing of the man who writes, at the moment that he writes, and thus is, it is here that, the daily work, the WORK, gets in, for only he, the man

III. PROJECTIVE VERSE

who writes, can declare, at every moment, the line, its metric and its ending – where its breathings shall come to, termination.

The trouble with most work, to my taking, since the breaking away from traditional lines and stanzas, and from such wholes as, say, Chaucer's TROILUS or S's LEAR, is: contemporary workers go lazy RIGHT HERE WHERE THE LINE IS BORN.

Let me put it baldly. The two halves are:

the HEAD, by way of the EAR, to the SYLLABLE
the HEART, by way of the BREATH, to the LINE

And the joker? that it is in the 1st half of the proposition that, in composing, one lets-it-rip; and that it is in the 2nd half, surprise, it is the LINE that's the baby that gets, as the poem is getting made, the attention, the control, that it is right here, in the line, that the shaping takes place, each moment of the going.

I am dogmatic, that the head shows in the syllable. The dance of the intellect is there, among them, prose or verse. Consider the best minds you know in this here business: where does the head show, is it not, precise, here, in the swift currents of the syllable? can't you tell a brain when you see what it does, just there? It is true, what the master says he picked up from Confusion: all the thots men are capable of can be entered on the back of a postage stamp. So, is it not the PLAY of a mind we are after, is not that that shows whether a mind is there at all?

And the threshing floor for the dance? Is it anything but the LINE? And when the line has, is, a deadness, is it not a heart which has gone lazy, is it not, suddenly, slow things, similes, say, adjectives, or such, that we are bored by?

For there is a whole flock of rhetorical devices which have now to be brought under a new bead, now that we sight with the line. Simile is only one bird who comes down, too easily. The descriptive functions generally have to be watched, every second, in projective verse, because of their easiness, and thus their drain on the energy which composition by field allows into a poem. *Any* slackness takes off attention, that crucial thing, from the job in hand, from the *push* of the line under hand at the moment, under the reader's eye, in his moment. Observation of any kind is, like argument in prose, properly previous to the act of the poem, and, if allowed in, must be so juxtaposed, apposed, set in, that it does not, for an instant, sap the going energy of the content toward its form.

It comes to this, this whole aspect of the newer problems. (We now enter, actually, the large area of the whole poem, into the FIELD, if you like, where all the syllables and all the lines must be managed in their relations to each other.) It is a matter, finally, of OBJECTS, what they are, what they are inside a poem, how they got there, and, once there, how they are to be used. This is something I want to get to in another way in Part II, but, for the moment, let me indicate this, that every element in an open poem (the syllable, the line, as well as the image, the sound, the sense) must be taken up as participants in the kinetic of the poem just as solidly as we are accustomed to take what we call the objects of reality; and that these elements are to be seen as creating the tensions of a poem just as totally as do those other objects create what we know as the world.

The objects which occur at every given moment of composition (of recognition, we can call it) are, can be, must be treated exactly as they do occur therein and not by any ideas or preconceptions from outside the poem, must be handled as a series of objects in field in such a way that a series of tensions (which they also are) are made to *hold,* and to hold exactly inside the content and the context of the poem which has forced itself, through the poet and them, into being.

Because breath allows *all* the speech-force of language back in (speech is the 'solid' of verse, is the secret of a poem's energy), because, now, a poem has, by speech, solidity, everything in it can now be treated as solids, objects, things; and, though insisting upon the absolute difference of the reality of verse from that other dispersed and distributed thing, yet each of these elements of a poem can be allowed to have the play of their separate energies and can be allowed, once the poem is well composed, to keep, as those other objects do, their proper confusions.

Which brings us up, immediately, bang, against tenses, in fact against syntax, in fact against grammar generally, that is, as we have inherited it. Do not tenses, must they not also be kicked around anew, in order that time, that other governing absolute, may be kept, as must the space-tensions of a poem, immediate, contemporary to the acting-on-you of the poem? I would argue that here, too, the LAW OF THE LINE, which projective verse creates, must be hewn to, obeyed, and that the conventions which logic has forced on syntax must be broken open as quietly as must the too set feet of the old line. But an analysis of how far a new poet can stretch the very conventions on which communication by language rests, is too big for these notes, which are meant, I hope it is obvious, merely to get things started.

Let me just throw in this. It is my impression that *all* parts of speech suddenly, in composition by field, are fresh for both sound and percussive use, spring up like unknown, unnamed vegetables in the patch, when you work it, come spring. Now take Hart Crane. What strikes me in him is the singleness of the push to the nominative, his push along that one arc of freshness, the attempt to get back to word as handle. (If logos is word as thought, what is word as noun, as, pass me that, as Newman Shea used to ask, at the galley table, put a jib on the blood, will ya.) But there is a loss in Crane of what Fenollosa is so right about, in syntax, the sentence as first act of nature, as lightning, as passage of force from subject to object, quick, in this case, from Hart to me, in every case, from me to you, the VERB, between two nouns. Does not Hart miss the advantages, by such an isolated push, miss the point of the whole front of syllable, line, field, and what happened to all language, and to the poem, as a result?

I return you now to London, to beginnings, to the syllable, for the pleasures of it, to intermit:

> If music be the food of love, play on,
> give me excess of it, that, surfeiting,
> the appetite may sicken, and so die.
> That strain again. It had a dying fall,
> o, it came over my ear like the sweet sound
> that breathes upon a bank of violets,
> stealing and giving odour.

What we have suffered from, is manuscript, press, the removal of verse from its producer and its reproducer, the voice, a removal by one, by two removes from its place of origin *and* its destination. For the breath has a double meaning which latin had not yet lost.

The irony is, from the machine has come one gain not yet sufficiently observed or used, but which leads directly on toward projective verse and its consequences. It is the advantage of the typewriter that, due to its rigidity and its space precisions, it can, for a poet, indicate exactly the breath, the pauses, the suspensions even of syllables, the juxtapositions even of parts of phrases, which he intends. For the first time the poet has the stave and the bar a musician has had. For the first time he can, without the convention of rime and meter, record the listening he has done to his own speech and by that one act indicate how he would want any reader, silently or otherwise, to voice his work.

It is time we picked the fruits of the experiments of Cummings, Pound, Williams, each of whom has, after his way, already used the machine as a scoring to his composing, as a script to its vocalization. It is now only a matter of the recognition of the conventions of composition by field for us to bring into being an open verse as formal as the closed, with all its traditional advantages.

If a contemporary poet leaves a space as long as the phrase before it, he means that space to be held, by the breath, an equal length of time. If he suspends a word or syllable at the end of a line (this was most Cummings' addition) he means that time to pass that it takes the eye – that hair of time suspended – to pick up the next line. If he wishes a pause so light it hardly separates the words, yet does not want a comma – which is an interruption of the meaning rather than the sounding of the line – follow him when he uses a symbol the typewriter has ready to hand:

'What does not change / is the will to change'

Observe him, when he takes advantage of the machine's multiple margins, to juxtapose:

'Sd he:
    to dream takes no effort
        to think is easy
            to act is more difficult

    but for a man to act after he has taken thought, this!
is the most difficult thing of all'

Each of these lines is a progressing of both the meaning and the breathing forward, and then a backing up, without a progress or any kind of movement outside the unit of time local to the idea.

There is more to be said in order that this convention be recognized, especially in order that the revolution out of which it came may be so forwarded that work will get published to offset the reaction now afoot to return verse to inherited forms of cadence and rime. But what I want to emphasize here, by this emphasis on the typewriter as the personal and instantaneous recorder of the poet's work, is the already projective nature of verse as the sons of Pound and Williams are practicing it. Already they are composing as though verse was to have the reading its writing involved, as though not the eye but the ear was to be its measurer, as though the intervals of its composition could be so carefully put down as to be precisely the intervals of its registration. For the ear, which once had the burden of memory to quicken it (rime & regular cadence were its aids and have merely lived on in print after the oral necessities were ended) can now again, that the poet has his means, be the threshold of projective verse.

II

Which gets us to what I promised, the degree to which the projective involves a stance toward reality outside a poem as well as a new stance towards the reality of a poem itself. It is a matter of content, the content of Homer or of Euripides or of Seami as distinct from that which I might call the more 'literary' masters. From the moment the projective purpose of the act of verse is recognized, the content does – it will – change. If the beginning and the end is breath, voice in its largest sense, then the material of verse shifts. It has to. It starts with the composer. The dimension of his line itself changes, not to speak of the change in his conceiving, of the matter he will turn to, of the scale in which he imagines that matter's use. I myself would pose the difference by a physical image. It is no accident that Pound and Williams both were involved variously in a movement which got called 'objectivism'. But that word was then used in some sort of a necessary quarrel, I take it, with 'subjectivism'. It is now too late to be bothered with the latter. It has excellently done itself to death, even though we are all caught in its dying. What seems to me a more valid formulation for present use is 'objectism', a word to be taken to stand for the kind of relation of man to experience which a poet might state as the necessity of a line or a work to be as wood is, to be as clean as wood is as it issues from the hand of nature, to be as shaped as wood can be when a man has had his hand to it. Objectism is the getting rid of the lyrical interference of the individual as ego, of the 'subject' and his soul, that peculiar presumption by which western man has interposed himself between what he is as a creature of nature (with certain instructions to carry out) and those other creations of nature which we may, with no derogation, call objects. For a man is himself an object, whatever he may take to be his advantages, the more likely to recognize himself as such the greater his advantages, particularly at that moment that he achieves an humilitas sufficient to make him of use.

It comes to this: the use of a man, by himself and thus by others, lies in how he conceives his relation to nature, that force to which he owes his somewhat small existence. If he sprawl, he shall find little to sing but himself, and shall sing, nature has such paradoxical ways, by way of artificial forms outside himself. But if he stays inside himself, if he is contained within his nature as he is participant in the larger force, he will be able to listen, and his hearing through himself will give him secrets objects share. And by an inverse law his shapes will make their own way. It is in this sense that the projective act, which is the artist's act in the larger field of objects, leads to dimensions larger than the man. For a man's problem, the moment he takes speech up in all its fullness, is to give his work his seriousness, a seriousness sufficient to cause the thing he makes to try to take its place alongside the things of nature. This is not easy. Nature works from reverence, even in her destructions (species go down with a crash). But breath is man's special qualification as animal. Sound is a dimension he has extended. Language is one of his proudest acts. And when a poet rests in these as they are in himself (in his physiology, if you like, but the life in him, for all that) then he, if he chooses to speak from these roots, works in that area where nature has given him size, projective size.

It is projective size that the play, 'The Trojan Women', possesses, for it is able to stand, is it not, as its people do, beside the Aegean – and neither Andromache or the sea suffer diminution. In a less 'heroic' but equally 'natural' dimension Seami causes the Fisherman and the Angel to stand clear in 'Hagoromo'. And Homer, who is such an unexamined cliche that I do not think I need to press home in what scale Nausicaa's girls wash their clothes.

Such works, I should argue – and I use them simply because their equivalents are yet to be done – could not issue from men who conceived verse without the full relevance of human voice, without reference to where lines come from, in the individual who writes. Nor do I think it accident that, at this end point of the argument, I should use, for examples, two dramatists and an epic poet. For I would hazard the guess that, if projective verse is practiced long enough, is driven ahead hard enough along the

III. PROJECTIVE VERSE

course I think it dictates, verse again can carry much larger material than it has carried in our language since the Elizabethans. But it can't be jumped. We are only at its beginnings, and if I think that the 'Cantos' make more 'dramatic' sense than do the plays of Mr. Eliot, it is not because I think they have solved the problem but because the methodology of the verse in them points a way by which, one day, the problem of larger content and of larger forms may be solved. Eliot is, in fact, a proof of a present danger, of 'too easy' a going on the practice of verse as it has been, rather than as it must be, practiced. There is no question, for example, that Eliot's line, from 'Prufrock' on down, has speech-force, is 'dramatic', is, in fact, one of the most notable lines since Dryden. I suppose it stemmed immediately to him from Browning, as did so many of Pound's early things. In any case Eliot's line has obvious relations backward to the Elizabethans, especially to the soliloquy. Yet O.M. Eliot is *not* projective. It could even be argued (and I say this carefully, as I have said all things about the non-projective, having considered how each of us must save himself after his own fashion and how much, for that matter, each of us owes to the non-projective, and will continue to owe, as both go alongside each other) but it could be argued that it is because Eliot has stayed inside the non-projective that he fails as a dramatist – that his root is the mind alone, and a scholastic mind at that (no high *intelletto* despite his apparent clarities) – and that, in his listenings he has stayed there where the ear and the mind are, has only gone from his fine ear outward rather than, as I say a projective poet will, down through the workings of his own throat to that place where breath comes from, where breath has its beginnings, where drama has to come from, where, the coincidence is, all act springs.

IV. Maximus (1): Polis

The early *Maximus* poems were written literally to Gloucester by Olson in his wanderings in the same way that Maximus, a second-century neo-Platonist, sent sermons back to his own city of Tyre. Olson confessed that Maximus was not as interesting as he had hoped, but he found the analogy useful, especially when he discovered that Tyre was the last hold-out against the steam-roller of Alexander the Great, just as he wished Gloucester on the island of Cape Ann might resist the inroads of what the rest of the nation had become:

> o tansy city, root city
> let them not make you
> as the nation is...

But polis, which in the Greek sense would be a city governed by citizens known to each other, neighbour accountable to neighbour, is not so easily defined today.

Gloucester, Mass.; view looking west from East Gloucester. Plate G from 'The Fishermen of the United States' by George Brown Goode and Joseph W. Collins, section IV of George Brown Goode (ed.), *The Fisheries and Fishery Industries of the United States* (US Commission of Fish and Fisheries, Washington DC: Government Printing Office 1887).

IV. MAXIMUS (1): POLIS

I speak to any of you, not to you all, to no group, not to you as citizens
as my Tyrian might have. Polis now
is a few, is a coherence not even yet new (the island of this city
is a mainland now of who? who can say who are
citizens?

Thus, 'Letter 3'. The rest of the poems of this section fill out what we can take to be Olson's tentative answer: 'Polis is eyes'.

Letter 3

Apparently the strong-smelling plant tansy was used on the early fishing boats as something of an air freshener. Olson thinks his city today could use some against the phoney 'mu-sick'. The particular thing which grated on Olson in this poem was a negative review the Gloucester paper gave to Vincent Ferrini's new little magazine, which contained two Olson poems. Of course, the philistine threat is seen in broader terms, the whole weight of the 'nation' pressing in on his polis of Gloucester, a working town with old-fashioned values.

Tansy buttons, tansy
for my city
Tansy for their noses

Tansy for them,
tansy for Gloucester to take the smell
of all owners,
the smell

Tansy
for all of us

>   Let those who use words cheap, who use us cheap
>   take themselves out of the way
>   Let them not talk of what is good for the city

>   Let them free the way for me, for the men of the Fort
>   who are not hired, who buy the white houses

>   Let them cease putting out words in the public print
>   so that any of us have to leave, so that my Portuguese leave,
>   leave the Lady they gave us, sell their schooners

    with the greyhounds aft, the long Diesels
    they put their money in, leave Gloucester
    in the present shame of,
    the wondership stolen by,
    ownership

Tansy from Cressy's
I rolled in as a boy
and didn't know it was
tansy

1

Did you know, she sd, growing up there,
how rare it was? And it turned out later she meant exactly the long field
drops down from Ravenswood where the land abrupts,
this side of Fresh Water Cove, and throws out
that wonder of my childhood, the descending green does run
so,
by the beach

        where they held the muster Labor Day, and the engine teams
        threw such arcs of water

                      runs with summer with
tansy

2

I was not born there, came, as so many of the people came,
from elsewhere. That is, my father did. And not from the Provinces,
not from Newfoundland. But we came early enough. When he came,
there were three hundred sail could fill the harbor,
if they were all in, as for the Races, say
Or as now the Italians are in, for San Pietro,
and the way it is from Town Landing, all band-concert,
and fireworks

IV. MAXIMUS (1): POLIS

So I answered her: Yes,
I knew (I had that to compare to it,
was Worcester)

As the people of the earth are now, Gloucester
is heterogeneous, and so can know polis
not as localism, not that mu-sick (the trick
of corporations, newspapers, slick magazines, movie houses,
the ships, even the wharves, absentee-owned

they whine to my people, these entertainers, sellers

they play upon their bigotries (upon their fears

these   they have the nerve
to speak of that lovely hour
the Waiting Station, 5 o'clock, the Magnolia bus, Al Levy
on duty (the difference
from 1 o'clock, all the women getting off
the Annisquam-Lanesville,
and the letter carriers

5:40, and only the lollers
in front of the shoe-shine parlor

these, right in the people's faces (and not at all as the gulls do it,
who do it straight, do it all over the 'Times' blowing
the day after, or the 'Summer Sun' catching on pilings, floating
off the Landing, the slime
the low tide reveals, the smell
then

3

The word does intimidate. The pay-check does.
But to use either, as cheap men

o tansy city, root city
let them not make you
as the nation is

I speak to any of you, not to you all, to no group, not to you as citizens
as my Tyrian might have. Polis now
is a few, is a coherence not even yet new (the island of this city
is a mainland now of who? who can say who are
citizens?

Only a man or a girl who hear a word
and that word meant to mean not a single thing the least more than
what it does mean (not at all to sell any one anything, to keep them
                                                                                 anywhere,
not even
in this rare place

      Root person in root place, hear one tansy-covered boy tell you
what any knowing man of your city might, a letter carrier, say,
or that doctor – if they dared afford to take the risk, if they reminded
                                                                  themselves
that you should not be played with, that you deserve... they'd tell you
the condition of the under-water, the cut-water of anyone, including those
who take on themselves
to give you advice,
to tell you, for example
what not to read

      They'd tell you, because they know (know as the house knows
wearing its white face, its clapboard mask) who there is will not outrage you
in the next edition, who'll not seek, even knowingly, to make you
slave

as he is slave
whom you read
as the bus starts off

                        whose slaver
                        would keep you off the sea, would keep you local,
                        my Nova Scotians,
                        Newfoundlanders,
                        Sicilianos,
                        Isolatos

4

Isolated person in Gloucester, Massachusetts, I, Maximus, address you
you islands
of men and girls

The Songs of Maximus

Olson was always poor. Echoing Gammer Girton's Needle, *a play he acted in in college, and the defiant song, 'Back and side go bare, go bare', these poems clearly intimate that he relished it. The simplicity of Innisfree appeals, as does the radicalness of Johnny Appleseed, the folk hero who spread liberality, the antithesis of the joint stock company. There is here a great regard for the Yankee spirit, Emerson's 'self-reliance', wherever it may be found. The 'lovely pedant' of 'Song 4' was the ichthyologist J.L.B. Smith of Rhodes University, South Africa, whose fifteen-year search for a coelacanth (a fish which flourished three million years ago) was rewarded in 1952 by a cable from Madagascar, from a*

The ichthyologist J.L.B. Smith and coelacanth, from a contemporary newspaper article, c. December 1952.

Captain Eric Hunt who had one on his deck injected with formaldehyde. He raced to the scene and, according to newspaper accounts that Olson read, was so overcome that he asked Hunt to unwrap it, then knelt on the deck and wept.

These songs have the traditional satire of the pastoral genre, the pipes of Pan a counterpoint to the piped music introduced at that time into the streetcars of Washington DC where Olson was living. He also sets his abrasive song against bureaucratic philanthropy or, as he phrased it in a letter, 'our resistance to good when it is exposed before us without its proper cloak' (CO/FB p. 110).

Song 1

           colored pictures
of all things to eat: dirty
postcards
       And words, words, words
all over everything
               No eyes or ears left
to do their own doings (all

invaded, appropriated, outraged, all senses

including the mind, that worker on what is
                          And that other sense
made to give even the most wretched, or any of us, wretched,
that consolation (greased
                lulled
even the street-cars

song

Song 2

       all
wrong
       And I am asked – ask myself (I, too, covered
with the gurry of it) where
shall we go from here, what can we do
when even the public conveyances
sing?

IV. MAXIMUS (1): POLIS

    how can we go anywhere,
even cross-town
        how get out of anywhere (the bodies
all buried
in shallow graves?

Song 3

    This morning of the small snow
I count the blessings, the leak in the faucet
which makes of the sink time, the drop
of the water on water as sweet
as the Seth Thomas
in the old kitchen
my father stood in his drawers to wind (always
he forgot the 30th day, as I don't want to remember
the rent
      a house these days
so much somebody else's,
especially,
Congoleum's

      Or the plumbing,
that it doesn't work, this I like, have even used paper clips
as well as string to hold the ball up And flush it
with my hand
         But that the car doesn't, that no moving thing moves
without that song I'd void my ear of, the musickracket
of all ownership...
        Holes
in my shoes, that's all right, my fly
gaping, me out
at the elbows, the blessing
        that difficulties are once more

      'In the midst of plenty, walk
      as close to
      bare
        In the face of sweetness,
    piss

>   In the time of goodness,
> go side, go
> smashing, beat them, go as
> (as near as you can
>
>   tear
>
> In the land of plenty, have
> nothing to do with it
>   take the way of
>   the lowest,
>   including
>   your legs, go
>   contrary, go
>
>   sing

Song 4

I know a house made of mud & wattles,
I know a dress just sewed
                    (saw the wind
blow its cotton
against her body
from the ankle
            so!
it was Nike

            And her feet: such bones
I could have had the tears
that lovely pedant had
who couldn't unwrap it himself, had to ask them to, on the schooner's deck

and he looked,
the first human eyes to look again
at the start of human motion (just last week
300,000,000 years ago

                    She
was going fast

across the square, the water
this time of year, that
scarce

And the fish

Song 5

I have seen faces of want
and have not wanted the FAO: Appleseed
's gone back to
what any of us
New England

Song 6

you sing, you

who also

wants

Letter 10

*It tickled Olson to learn that Gloucester's first fishing stage (1623) had been exactly where his own family cottage had been located. He enjoyed pointing out to his friend Joyce Benson (*Selected Letters, *p. 371) that this was just at 'the ear of the g of Stage Head' on the back cover of* The Maximus Poems *(1960), while his present house at 28 Fort Square was 'on the dot exactly of the i in Point in Fort Point' on the front cover, from which vantage he could view his boyhood playground and the first settlement.*

He was also pleased, as this poem attests, that Gloucester was not founded as a Puritan camp but with the very practical purpose of enabling the fishermen to wait out the winter until the next fishing season when the boats returned, rather than having to return to Europe. In other words, it was in the tradition of economic betterment, not the Mayflower *strain of imported theocracy – that is, until 1629, when Endecott consolidated his church. The first working town of Gloucester was that short-lived, the power struggle so unbalanced, as to remind*

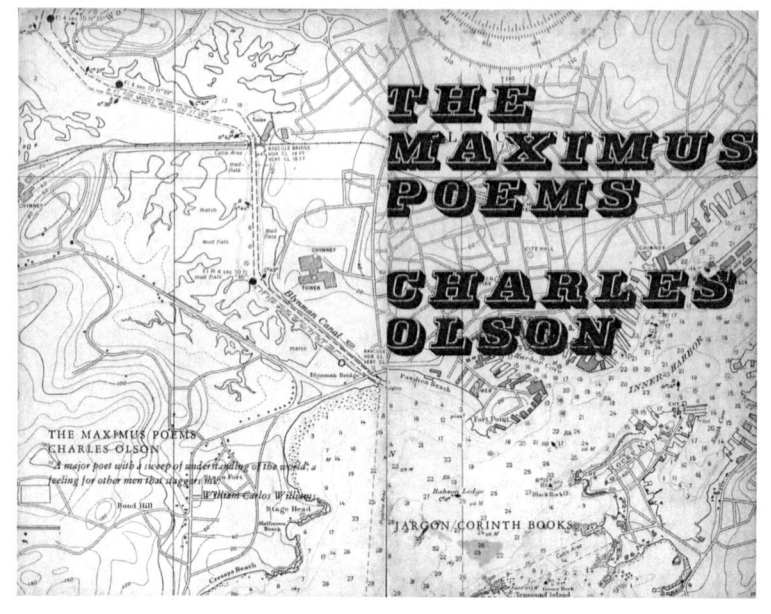

Cover of *The Maximus Poems* (New York: Jargon/Corinth 1960), showing map of Gloucester, Mass.

*Olson of his own time. Then, the hero was Roger Conant, who resisted; the later villain was James Conant, president of Harvard 1933–53 and High Commissioner to West Germany, a 'stooge' in the creation of a 'false state' (*Muthologos *1.115).*

on John White / on cod, ling, and poor-john

on founding: was it puritanism,
or was it fish?

And how, now, to found, with the sacred & the profane – both of them –
wore out

      The beak's
there. And the pectoral.
The fins,
for forwarding.

IV. MAXIMUS (I): POLIS

But to do it anew, now that even fishing...

1

It was fishing was first. Only after (Naumkeag) was it the other thing,
                   and Conant
would have nothing to do with it, went over to Beverly, to Bass River, to
                      keep clear
(as a later Conant I know has done the opposite, has not
kept clear)

It is a sign, that first house, Roger Conant's, there, Stage Fort. One of
                 Endecott's first acts
was to have it dragged to Salem for his own mansion, for the big house,
the frame of it was that sound, that handsome, the old carpentry

    (not the house-making I feel closest to, what followed, so close
    I'd sing, today, of Anne Bradstreet's,
    or any of them, Georgetown, Rowley, Ipswich,
    how private they are in their clapboards
    and yet how they thrust, sit there
    as strong as any building)

           Conant's
was Tudor

    Gloucester, your first house was as Elizabeth's
England

(and that that Endecott, the 'New', should have used it
inside of which to smile, and bless that covenant Higginson and the
                    others...

It sat
where my own house has been (where I am
founded

by racks so poor of fish there was not take enough to pay the Adventurers
                 back. Three years,
and their 3000 £ gone. And as much more again (where I have picked
                    coins up,

after circuses, slid out of men's trousers they so twisted in the bleacher seats
from the tricks Clyde Beatty made lions do,
keeping them under his eye and under his whip

3

Elizabeth dead,
and Tudor went to James
(as quick as Conant's house
was snatched to Salem

As you did not go,
Gloucester: you tipped, you were our
scales

>   (as I have been witness,
>   in my time,
>   to all slide
>   national, international,
>   even learning slide
>
>   by the acts of another Conant than he who left his Tudor house,
>   left fishing,
and lost everything to Endecott, lost the colony
to the first of,
the shrinkers

4

Now all things
are true by inverse:
religion
shrank Elizabeth's, money
dilates ours. Harvard
owns too much

>   and so its President
>   after destroying its localism ('meatballs',
>   they called the city fellers, the public school

IV. MAXIMUS (I): POLIS 63

    graduates) Conant destroyed Harvard
    by asking Oregon
    to send its brightest

Roger Conant did not destroy, was, in fact, himself destroyed, as was the
                                                                          city, 1626

        and is paid off by those he served (State St., Washington), is made
                                                                            High Commissioner
    (Endecott, of a stooge State

my Conant
only removed to 'Beggarly',
as the smug of Salem – the victors! –
called that place still is, for me
(when I go down 1 A or take the train
the opening out
of my countree

Capt Christopher Levett (of York)

It is understood that the Maximus *poems had their inception when Olson was visiting Gloucester in June 1947 and, after a lunch with the local historian Alfred Mansfield Brooks, went right out to buy a copy of John J. Babson's* History of the Town of Gloucester *(1860). After he settled in Fort Point in August 1957, Olson began to crack open his history books in earnest. The facts and quotations that make up this poem were culled from Levett's published account of his landing at Maine in 1624 and building a house, naming it York after his birthplace. Levett and Roger Conant and John Smith were the people who captured Olson's imagination. The second and successive waves of colonists were a different matter.*

                        Levett is a measure
                        – the writ, that 14 men
                        had sat down
                        at Cape Anne, did not run
                        to him, where Portland

was to be; and didn't get
to London, from the West
country. Levett says only,
1624, I left
some men myself, and Plymouth

people fish… Though that
Cape Ann led on
to Commonwealth, and Maine
stayed Maine,
is not the news. The news

which Levett had to tell
(as Conant might have)
was a simpler thing, of such import
an island's named today
'House Island' – and Conant's

house was timbers
in a city's stable
so few years back
I touched them, when a kid,
and didn't know it, the first ones

on a continent which men
have let go so our
eyes which look
to strike
take nothing

of even furthest previous
thought, local
national or new spatial

as tolerable. A man
who speaks as Levett does
of what he's done
('I have obtained a place
of habitation in New-

England, where I have built
a house, and fortified it
in a reasonable good fashion,
strong enough against such enemies
as are those Savage people')

speaks (as he does of each
new thing he saw and did
in these new parts) so we,
who live at this poor end
of goods, & thing, & men,

when materials, of each,
are such a man can't eat
sleep walk move go
apart from his own dwelling,
the dirtiness of goodness

cheapness shit is
upon the world. We'll turn
to keep our house, turn to
houses where our kind,
and hungry after them,

not willing to bear one short walk
more out into even what they've done
to earth itself, find
company. Since these two men
put down two houses

by fish flakes and stages
on rocks near water with trees
against sea – one's forced,
considering America,
to a single truth: the newness

the first men knew was almost
from the start dirtied
by second comers. About seven years
and you can carry cinders
in your hand for what

America was worth. May she be damned
for what she did so soon
to what was such a newing
that we, who out the side
of her come (have cut ourselves

out of her drugstore flattened-hillside gut
like Wash-Ching-Geka cut
the Winnebago nation out
of elephant – 'the fish,
sd Levett, which we there saw,

some with wings, others with manes,
ears, heads, who chased
one another with open mouths
like stone Horses in a parcke' –
We have the gain. We know

what Levett Smith or Conant
didn't, that no one
knew better
than to cash in on it. Out,
is the cry of a coat of wonder

Maximus to Gloucester, Letter 27 [withheld]

Why was this poem 'withheld' from the 1960 Maximus volume? Perhaps because Olson was not ready to declare how much of an influence Alfred North Whitehead had become, intervening, as it were, in the historical narrative. Putting together a second Maximus volume in 1963, Olson might have seen, considering the direction the poem had gone, that 'Letter 27' represented a necessary leap forward to establish the personal in the poem. Olson had been struck by a certain passage in Whitehead's Adventures of Ideas *(1933) which asserted: 'It was the defect of the Greek analysis of generation that it conceived it in terms of the bare incoming of novel abstract form... In addition to the notions of the welter of events and of the forms which they illustrate, we require a third term, personal history.' This quotation allowed the poet (or Maximus Americanus) to assert his uniqueness. Reinforced, he straightens his back and returns to the task of forging a polis.*

I come back to the geography of it,
the land falling off to the left
where my father shot his scabby golf
and the rest of us played baseball
into the summer darkness until no flies
could be seen and we came home
to our various piazzas where the women
buzzed

To the left the land fell to the city,
to the right, it fell to the sea

I was so young my first memory
is of a tent spread to feed lobsters
to Rexall conventioneers, and my father,
a man for kicks, came out of the tent roaring
with a bread-knife in his teeth to take care of
a druggist they'd told him had made a pass at
my mother, she laughing, so sure, as round
as her face, Hines pink and apple,
under one of those frame hats women then

This, is no bare incoming
of novel abstract form, this

is no welter or the forms
of those events, this,

Greeks, is the stopping
of the battle

      It is the imposing
of all those antecedent predecessions, the precessions

of me, the generation of those facts
which are my words, it is coming

from all that I no longer am, yet am,
the slow westward motion of

more than I am

There is no strict personal order

for my inheritance.

      No Greek will be able

to discriminate my body.

      An American

is a complex of occasions,

themselves a geometry

of spatial nature.

      I have this sense,

IV. MAXIMUS (1): POLIS

that I am one

with my skin

Plus this – plus this:

that forever the geography

which leans in

on me I compel

backwards I compel   Gloucester

to yield, to

change

      Polis

is this

V. In Thicket

Olson and Constance Wilcock had lived together as man and wife (though without benefit of marriage licence) for about nine years when fate took a turn and the fan letters of divorcée Frances Boldereff, begun in November 1947, finally touched him. It was another year before they met with intent, and still another six months before he realised what he had got himself into. In spite of, or because of, the pain, this love triangle caused Olson to write one of his greatest poems, 'In Cold Hell, in Thicket'.

He and Frances met on only a handful of occasions, Olson clearly preferring to write letters. The story is told in full in *Charles Olson and Frances Boldereff: A Modern Correspondence* (Middletown, Conn.: Wesleyan University Press, 1999). Frances finally blew a fuse on 3 September 1950 and Olson was free, free to take Connie to Mexico, where they conceived a child. With the birth of Kate in October 1951, the new triangle laid the old one to rest. At least for a time.

La Chute

In late May 1949 Frances Boldereff sent Olson an offprint she had acquired by visiting the scholar S.N. Kramer at the University of Pennsylvania. It was 'The Epic of Gilgameš and its Sumerian Sources', reprinted from the Journal of the American Oriental Society *64 (1944), pp. 7–23. No woman had ever been so alert to Olson's susceptibilities. He wrote 'La Chute' the next day, carefully adapting from Kramer's translation lines which might or might not appear to be an overt invitation.*

LA CHUTE

O my drum, hollowed out thru the thin slit,
carved from the cedar wood, the base I took
when the tree was felled
                                    o my lute
wrought from the tree's crown

my drum whose lustiness
was not to be resisted

my lute from whose pulsations
not one could turn away
                                    They
are where the dead are
                      my drum
fell where the dead are, who
will bring it up, my lute
who will bring it up
where it fell in the face of them
where they are, where my lute and drum

have fallen?

In Cold Hell, in Thicket

With 'Ya, selva oscura', we are directed to the opening lines of Dante's Inferno, *translated in the Temple Classics prose: 'In the middle of the journey of our life I came to myself in a dark wood [selva oscura] where the straight way was lost.' Alternatively, one could summarise this mid-life crisis as the heavens having fallen. In Egyptian cosmology the sky goddess Nut was arched to form the heavens, with the stars on her underside. The earth-god Geb is often depicted reclining effortlessly beneath her. The poem is recording Connie's withdrawal of this protection. But Olson, to regain his ease, cannot make the simple move of cutting out the third party of the triangle. Thus he has to face up to crossing and recrossing the battlefield of his own bones, wavering and, since he is a poet, living in precise knowledge of his wavering.*

In cold hell, in thicket, how
abstract (as high mind, as not lust, as love is) how
strong (as strut or wing, as polytope, as things are
constellated) how
strung, how cold
can a man stay (can men) confronted
thus?

All things are made bitter, words even
are made to taste like paper, wars get tossed up
like lead soldiers used to be
(in a child's attic) lined up
to be knocked down, as I am,
by firings from a spit-hardened fort, fronted
as we are, here, from where we must go

God, that man, as his acts must, as there is always
a thing he can do, he can raise himself, he raises
on a reed he raises his

Or, if it is me, what
he has to say

V. IN THICKET

1
What has he to say?
In hell it is not easy
to know the traceries, the markings
(the canals, the pits, the mountings by which space
declares herself, arched, as she is, the sister,
awkward stars drawn for teats to pleasure him, the brother
who lies in stasis under her, at ease as any monarch or
a happy man

How shall he who is not happy, who has been so made unclear,
who is no longer privileged to be at ease, who, in this brush, stands
reluctant, imageless, unpleasured, caught in a sort of hell, how
shall he convert this underbrush, how turn this unbidden place
how trace and arch again
the necessary goddess?

2
The branches made against the sky are not of use, are
already done, like snow-flakes, do not, cannot service
him who has to raise   (Who puts this on, this damning of his flesh?)
he can, but how far, how sufficiently far can he raise the thickets of
this wilderness?

> How can he change, his question is
> these black and silvered knivings, these
> awkwardnesses?
>
> How can he make these blood-points into panels, into sides
> for a king's, for his own
> for a wagon, for a sleigh, for the beak of, the running sides of
> a vessel fit for
> moving?
>
> How can he make out, he asks,
> of this low eye-view,
> size?
>
> And archings traced and picked enough to hold
> to stay, as she does, as he, the brother, when,
> here where the mud is, he is frozen, not daring

>   where the grass grows, to move his feet from fear
>   he'll trespass on his own dissolving bones, here
>   where there is altogether too much remembrance?

3
The question, the fear he raises up himself against
(against the same each act is proffered, under the eyes
each fix, the town of the earth over, is managed) is: Who
am I?

Who am I but by a fix, and another,
a particle, and the congery of particles carefully picked one by another,

>   as in this thicket, each
>   smallest branch, plant, fern, root
>   – roots lie, on the surface, as nerves are laid open –
>   must now (the bitterness of the taste of her) be
>   isolated, observed, picked over, measured, raised
>   as though a word, an accuracy were a pincer!
>   this
>   is the abstract, this
>   is the cold doing, this
>   is the almost impossible

>   So shall you blame those
>   who give it up, those who say
>   it isn't worth the struggle?

>   (Prayer
>   Or a death as going over to – shot by yr own forces – to
>   a greener place?

>   Neither
>   any longer
>   usable)

>   By fixes only (not even any more by shamans)
>   can the traceries
>   be brought out

V. IN THICKET

II

ya, selva oscura, but hell now
is not exterior, is not to be got out of, is
the coat of your own self, the beasts
emblazoned on you   And who
can turn this total thing, invert
and let the ragged sleeves be seen
by any bitch or common character?   Who
can endure it where it is, where the beasts are met,
where yourself is, your beloved is, where she
who is separate from you, is not separate, is not
goddess, is, as your core is,
the making of one hell
                        where she moves off, where she is
                        no longer arch

    (this is why he of whom we speak does not move, why
    he stands so awkward where he is, why
    his feet are held, like some ragged crane's
    off the nearest next ground, even from
    the beauty of the rotting fern his eye
    knows, as he looks down, as,
    in utmost pain if cold can be so called,
    he looks around this battlefield, this
    rotted place where men did die, where boys
    and immigrants have fallen, where nature
    (the years that she's took over)
    does not matter, where
                           that men killed, do kill, that woman kills
                          is part, too, of his question

2
That it is simple, what the difference is –
that a man, men, are now their own wood
and thus their own hell and paradise
that they are, in hell or in happiness, merely
something to be wrought, to be shaped, to be carved, for use, for
others

does not in the least lessen his, this unhappy man's
obscurities, his
confrontations

He shall step, he
will shape, he
is already also
moving off
             into the soil, on to his own bones

he will cross
             (there is always a field,
               for the strong there is always
               an alternative)
                          But a field
               is not a choice, is
               as dangerous as a prayer, as a death, as any
               misleading, lady

He will cross
             And is bound to enter (as she is)
             a later wilderness.
                          Yet
             what he does here, what he raises up
             (he must, the stakes are such
                                 this at least
             is a certainty, this
             is a law, is not one of the questions, this
             is what was talked of as
             – what was it called, demand?)

He will do what he now does, as she will, do
carefully, do
without wavering,
without
             as even the branches,
               even in this dark place, the twigs
                                 how
               even the brow
of what was once to him a beautiful face

as even the snow-flakes waver in the light's eye

             as even forever wavers (gutters
               in the wind of loss)

even as he will forever waver

precise as hell is, precise
as any words, or wagon,
can be made

The Ring of

This poem was written a week or so before the birth of Kate, therefore we cannot strictly say it is a celebration of that event. In anticipation of the joy, it is a general hymn to love as the active element in creativity, though Aphrodite as muse is not an easy option, as Olson, one of the 'lovers of the difficult', the previous year found out.

    it was the west wind caught her up, as
    she rose
    from the genital
    wave, and bore her from the delicate
    foam, home
    to her isle

    and those lovers
    of the difficult, the hours
    of the golden day welcomed her, clad her, were
    as though they had made her, were wild
    to bring this new thing born
    of the ring of the sea pink
    & naked, this girl, brought her
    to the face of the gods, violets
    in her hair

    Beauty, and she
    said no to zeus & them all, all were not or
    was it she chose the ugliest
    to bed with, or was it straight
    and to expiate the nature of beauty, was it?

knowing hours, anyway,
she did not stay long, or the lame
was only one part, & the handsome
mars had her   And the child
had that name, the arrow of
as the flight of, the move of
his mother who adorneth

with myrtle the dolphin and words
they rise, they do who
are born of like
elements

VI. Outside the Box

It was in trying to distinguish himself from Ezra Pound that Olson used the term 'Western Box': 'Gemisto, 1429 A.D. up' (*Selected Writings*, p. 129). Olson claimed for himself a wider chronological territory: back to Sumer and forward into a non-euclidean reality yet to be fully delineated. The new coherence would be a contrary to Sigismundo Malatesta, John Adams, or any other hero whose ego Pound felt matched his own.

Olson got a chance to go physically 'outside the box' when he found he could cash a couple of hundred dollars of post office retirement money and spend six months in the Yucatan. He could not afford Mesopotamia to test out the perceptions he had put into 'The Gate and the Center'. The letters he sent from Lerma, Campeche, to Robert Creeley, and edited by him as *Mayan Letters* (1953), remain the chief document of Olson's discovery of the living archaic that infuses his notion of the post-modern.

Perry Anderson's *The Origins of Postmodernity* (1998) confirms that Olson was the first literary figure to use the term 'post-modern' (preceded only by the historian Arnold Toynbee), but it should be stressed that Olson's post-modernism (unlike all subsequent definitions of it) calls on us to make such use of the past that we become roundly at home in the universe.

The Gate & the Center

Most of Olson's essays had their first statement in private letters. In the exingencies of life, and by the rule that first expression is probably the best, they usually came to publication without much revision. 'The Gate & the Center' retains the feel of looking over the writer's shoulder at the moment the ideas were ignited. For his proposed little magazine, Robert Creeley had requested something from Olson on the subject of education. This is the best Olson can do as of 1950: 'if it ain't all that's in my mind, it's nice to spill this, at least, for what it is, right now' (unpublished letter at Stanford).

1:

What I am kicking around is this notion: that KNOWLEDGE either goes for the CENTER or it's inevitably a State Whore – which American and Western education generally is, has been, since its beginning. (I am flatly taking Socrates as the progenitor, his methodology still the RULE: 'I'll stick my logic up, and classify, boy, classify you right out of existence.')

So when I say, it's a question of re-establishing a concept of knowledge as culture rather than a question of what's wrong with the schools, I mean that already anyone who wants to begin to get straight has to, to start, a straight man has to uneducate himself first, in order to begin to pick up, to take up, to get back, in order to get on. Which is turkey-crazy, is it not? So I say, let's take the question by another handle, let's say some simple and non-aesthetic propositions: what is the story of man, the FACTS, where did he come from, when did he invent a city, what did a plateau have to do with it, or a river valley? what foods were necessary (I am thinking here of Stefansson on diets, Carl Sauer on starch crops and how, where they could be domesticated)

were the people on the edge of the retreating ice, marauders, or were they (as Sauer so beautifully argues) fisher-folk? and man's first food clue, that tubers which poisoned fish did not poison humans?

and are euhemerists like myself (so I am told ISHMAEL proves me) correct, that gods are men first? and how many generations does it take to turn a hero into a god? is it 3 (ex., A. Lincoln)?

1000 more such questions, put straight down the alley, without deference to arbitrary divisions of 'learning' which are calculated, are purposely brought into being (Old Stink Sock on down) to CONFUSE confuse CONFOUND

Take language (& start with Fenollosa): did anyone tell you – same anyones are so stuck with variants – that all Indo-European language (ours) appears to stem from the very same ground on which the original agglutinative language was invented, Sumeria? and that our language can be seen to hold in itself now as many of those earliest elements as it does Sanskrit roots? that though some peoples stuck to the signs while others took off with the sounds, both the phonetic and ideographic is still present and available for use as impetus and explosion in our alphabetic speech? (Why Fenollosa wrote the damned best piece on language since when, is because, in setting Chinese directly over against American, he reasserted these resistant primes in our speech, put us back to the origins of their force not as history but as living oral law to be discovered in speech as directly as it is in our mouths.)

It is one of the last acts of liberation that science has to offer, that is, modern science stemming from the Arabs, that all the real boys, today, are spending their time no longer alone but in teams, because they have found out that the problem now is not what things are so much as it is what happens BETWEEN things, in other words:
COMMUNICATION (why we are at ripe, live center) – and the joker? that from Stockpile Szilard on down, what the hot lads are after (under him at Chicago, Merritt at Columbia, Theodore Vann at the Univ. of Paris, and at the Princeton Institute) is, what is it in the *human* organism, what is the wave (is it H-mu) that makes communication possible! It kills me. And I made one physicist run, when I sd, quite quietly, the only thing wrong with yr teams is, you have left out the one professional who has been busy abt this problem all the time the rest of you and yr predecessors have been fingering that powerful solid, but useless when abstraction, Nature.

Item: to answer all who say, but is a poet that important? Edith Porada, in – get this – Corpus of Ancient Near Eastern Seals in North American Collections, Edited for the Committee of Ancient Near Eastern Seals, a Project of the Iranian Institute, the Oriental Institute of the Univ. of Chicago and the Yale Babylonian Collection, Bollingen Series XLV (I find that she says this not in the above but in *Mesopotamian Art in Cylinder Seals of the Pierpont Morgan Libraries*, N.Y., 1947, p. 1):

'Sometimes foreign influences were introduced through trade, sometimes through contact with the many peoples who time and again invaded the rich Mesopotamian plain from the poorer and less civilized regions of the East, North, and West. Moreover, while the actual assumption of power by a foreign king in Mesopotamia was a sudden event, marking the climax of an invasion, such invasions were often preceded by the gradual infiltration of foreigners into the country as mercenaries or laborers. The new element therefore made itself felt gradually, and a sudden break in the artistic development never took place, only the disintegration of one style and the emergence of another. It may be added that artists appear to have been so highly valued that they were spared in warfare.'

Well, to hell with it, only – as I sd before – the poet is the only pedagogue left, to be trusted. And I mean the tough ones, only the very best, not the bulk of them and the other educators.

Which brings us home. To Porada, & S. N. Kramer's translations of the city poems, add one L. A. Waddell. What Waddell gives me is this chronology: that, from 3378 BC (date man's 1st city, name and face of creator also known) in unbroken series first at Uruk, then from the sea-port Lagash out into colonies in the Indus Valley and, circa 2500, the Nile, until date 1200 BC or thereabouts, civilization had ONE CENTER, Sumer, in all directions, that this one people held such exact and superior force that all peoples around them were sustained by it, nourished, increased, advanced, that a city was a coherence which, for the first time since the ice, gave man the chance to join knowledge to culture and, with this weapon, shape dignities of economics and value sufficient to make daily life itself a dignity and a sufficiency.

(*Note:* I am the more convinced by this argument, that I have for some years, by way of Bérard, Herodotus, & Strzygowski (Frobenius au fond with his sun-moon, landfolk-seafolk premises) felt that it was just about 1200 BC that something broke, that a bowl went smash, and that, as a consequence, this artificial business of the 'East' and the 'West' came into its most false being.)

2:

Suddenly, by such a smallness of time, seen as back there 3378 to 2500 BC, the nature of life then is made available, seems suddenly not at all history, seems what it was, men falling off the original impetus but still close enough to the climax of a will to cohere to know what CENTER was, and, though going down hill, still keeping the FORCE, even though the SHAPE was starting even then to lose its sharpness.

((One may see the far end of the personages, events & acts of these years in such things as the Odyssey, Herakles, Egyptian folk tales (as Maspero gives them), Phoenician periploi, and Ionian thought. That the art of classical Egypt and Greece are also signs of this derivation is more obvious, now that Crete, Susa and even such a late thing as Dura-Europos are available. (We are only just beginning to gauge the backward of literature, breaking through the notion that Greece began it, to the writings farther back: to the Phoenicians, to the Babylonians, behind them the Akkadians, and, most powerful of all, the Sumerian poets, those first makers, better than 2000 years prior to Homer, Hesiod & Herodotus.)

VI. OUTSIDE THE BOX

When I say gauge, I am thinking that we have no measure of what men are capable of, taking, say, the 700 years from, say, Dante, as comparison of like time to what those men were about in the first 700 years of the Sumer thrust.

What I am trying to track down is, heroism. There has been, of course, no reason why, since Dante, that men should not have taken heroism solely in terms of man's capacity to overthrow or dominate external reality. Yet I do not for a minute think that this is – or will be – the gauge of a life turning on the SINGLE CENTER. But just because of our own late, & Western, impression we continue to shy, in our present disgust with such muscularity, away from all such apparent magnifications as epic and myths seem to include.

But the thing goes farther, & deeper. What has been these last 700 years, is the inevitable consequence of a contrary will to that of Sumer, a will which overcame the old will approximately 2500 BC and succeeded in making itself boss approximately 1200 BC. It is the long reach of this second will of man which we have known, the dead end of which we are the witnesses of. And the only answer of man to the rash of multiples which that wish to disperse causeth to break out (the multiple face of it, the swarming snake-choices it breeds as multiple as hairs) was one thing only, the only thing man had to put against it: the egocentric concept, a man himself as, and only contemporary to himself, the PROOF of anything, himself responsible only to himself by the exhibition of his energy, AHAB, end.

I pick up from the Omahas, to venture to see what happens ahead if I am right that now, only, once again, and only a second time, is the FIRST WILL back in business. A boy (or a girl, if she chose, though it was not required of the girl as it was of the boy) went out at 16, 17, alone into the woods, with nothing to take care of living, for three days of hunger & watch. The one end was, to woo a dream, and that dream, once it came, was, whatever its form, to be thereafter the SIGNATURE of that individual's life. What the boy or girl was not to do, was to speak of it. But due to the other part of the ceremony, which was to wear, from then on, a fetish to stand for the dream, it became possible for the individual instantly to know others of the tribe who had a like dream and to consort with same, as they thereafter did.

I should, myself, assume that both parts of this act rested on good cause, that whatever be individuation, there are groupings of us which create kin ('hungry after my own kind'), limits – of, say, Seven Tribes of man, or whatever – which same limits become vessels of behaviour towards *use* of self, & recognition.

It is in some such frame that the old human science of archetype figure and archetype event became relevant to individual behaviour at all time forward. And it would be my guess that we have been running, know it or not, on the invention of – the verbal function is not quite right: the recognition, obedience to, and creation of – just such archetypes by the Sumerians some time before and some certain time after 3378 BC (the date 2500 is only the outside limit this side of the action). And that, of course, we long ago lost the POINT & PURPOSE of what we call – and thus kill – the act of myth.

I have this dream, that just as we cannot now see & say the size of these early HUMAN KINGS, we cannot, by the very lost token of their science, see what size man can be once more capable of, once the turn of the flow of his energies that I speak of as the WILL TO COHERE is admitted, and its energy taken up.

What I should like to dispose of is, that it is a dream, any more than that, what I think we shall be able soon to demonstrate, the so-called figures & stories of the old science were never men. And I venture to say that their enlarged dimensions are no where near as discrepant from them as they were as we, going by what we have been able to see of man in recent time, including ourselves, would surmise.

The proposition is a simple one (and the more easily understood now that we have been shocked at what we did not know nature's energies capable of, generally): energy is larger than man, but therefore, if he taps it as it is in himself, his uses of himself are EXTENSIBLE in human directions & degree not recently granted. Quickly, therefore, the EXCEPTIONAL man, the 'hero', loses his description as 'genius' – his 'birth' is mere instrumentation for application to the energy he did not create – and becomes, instead, IMAGE of possibilities implicit in the energy, given the METHODOLOGY of its use by men from the man who is capable precisely of this, and only this kind of, intent & attention.

I am struck (as Waddell tells the stories of these men who were heroes who became gods) by the premises on which they acted, were expected to act, & were judged. And how very small, how hairlike, the difference is from the premises we have regarded, in our inherited blindness due to departure from the old science, as essential. For example, this, from a monument of Sargon of Agade, on the duties of a ruler, apparently formulated by his tutor (his 'Aristotle' or 'Apollonius of Tyana'), a man variously known as Annaki or Urura (Sanskrit: Aurva or Urva) date 2725 BC:

'arms' are allowable only as PROTECTION OF THE EARTH (I judge, in distinction from the ruler's power, or even the 'people's', in the sense of volk or nation). In fact, the next sentence of the inscription repeats the injunction thus:

THE GUARDIANSHIP OF THE EARTH IS THE RULER'S ESPECIAL PROVINCE.

And a later priest-king (whose statue-portraits in diorite & lapis-lazuli are straight projections of Gotama Buddha's face, the man Gotama), by name GUDA, King of the port Lagash, date 2370 BC, in reporting his accomplishments due to the restoration of the law codes of both the founder of that City, Uruash (c.3000), and of the patron of the city, Nimirrud (Nimrod), says this:

> the maid is now the equal of her mistress,
> the master & the slave consort as friends,
> the powerful & the humble lay down, side by side.

The whole question & continuing struggle to remain civilized Sumer documented in & out: I imagine you know the subtle tale of how Gilgamesh (King 14, and founder of the sea-dynasty of Sumeria, according to Waddell's count) was sent the rude fellow Enkidu to correct him because he, even Gilgamesh, had become a burden, in his lust, to his city's people. As I read it, it is an incredibly accurate myth of what happens to the best of men when they lose touch with the primordial & phallic energies & methodologies which, said this predecessor people of ours, make it possible for man, that participant thing, to take up, straight, nature's, live nature's force.

from Mayan Letters

The selection here, about half the letters Olson sent to Creeley between February and July 1951 (as published in Mayan Letters*), might just be enough to give the flavour of the adventure it was for Olson and his wife to be in Mexico for six months. It seeks to include the main illuminations that being 'offshore' provided to the 'archeologist of [the post-modern] morning'. On the eve of his departure for the Yucatan, Olson felt it important to communicate his motives to an ally in Germany, Rainer Gerhardt, in a letter of 15 January 1951 (*Selected Letters*, p. 125):*

> I am leaving tonight for my first vacation in 7 yrs. (On top of that it will be the 1st time I have been out of the States in 22 years!!) My wife and I are moving by bus to New Orleans, and, there, by a Norwegian freighter across the Gulf to Yucatan, specifically, Lerma, just outside Campeche. For, this MOVE, represents, god help me, some sort of a huge passage out… I feel finished with the frame of my people – that is, as an urgent necessity for me to come to conclusion about it (CALL ME ISHMAEL, surely, was a document of that struggle. And so much of the verse – KINGFISHERS, e.g.). And I go off with an ease and a joy and a hunger which surprises and delights me!

1

saturday feb 18 (is it?)　　　　　　　　　　lerma, campeche, mexico

Birds, lad: my god what birds. Last evening a thing like our hawk. And that woman of mine (again) most alert to their nature. It happened this way. I was down the beach bargaining to buy a piece of their best fish here, what sounds like madrigal, only it comes out smedreegal. I had my back turned no more than three minutes, when, turning, to come back to the house (Con was on the terraza out over the sea, surrounded by a dozen of these gabbling kids), below her, on the water line, I noticed these huge wings fluttering wrong. My guess was, one of the kids, all of whom carry sling-shots, had brought down a zopalote (our vulture, 'brother v,' as Con named them). But when I came near, I noticed, just as Con cried down, that it was no vulture but another bird which is quite beautiful here, in Maya a chii-mi (chee-me): flies in flock over the waterline, soaring like hawks, high, and is marked by a long splittail ((by god, i was right: just checked dictionary, and is, as I thought, our frigate bird))

　　　　　　　　　　there it was, poor chii-mi, stoned

by one of these little bastards, and the others, throwing more stones at it, and a couple, kicking it. And it working those three foot wings, hard, but not wild: very sure of itself, tho downed. By the time I came up, it had managed to get itself over, and was already out into the water, to get away from the kids. But each wave was wetting it down, and the misery was, that it drown.

My assumption was, the stone had broken its wing. But Con had seen it happen, and seems to have known it was only its head that had been struck (it was out cold, she told me later, for a minute or so, and then, on its back, had disgorged its last fish). Anyhow she had the brains to send down one of the older boys to bring it out of the water, and up on the terraza. And when I came up there it was, quiet, looking hard at everyone, with its gular pouch swollen like my Aunt Vandla's goiter, and its eye, not at all as a bird's is, when it is scared, or as, so quickly, they weaken and that film drops over the eye. Not at all: this chii-mi was more like an animal, in its strength. Yet I still thought it was done for, something in the wings gone.

Just about then it started to work its way forward, pulling its wings in to its body, and making it look so much more like, say, a duck. What it had in mind, was to try to lift itself the two feet up to the wall that goes round the terraza. But it could not. It had worked itself into the inner angle of a corner. So I reached down and raised the right wing up to the top of the wall. Then the left. And itself, it pulled its body up, perched for an instant, and swung off, off and up, into the sky, god help us, up and out over the sea, higher and higher, and, not like the others but working its wings in shorter, quicker strokes, it pulled off and off, out over the shrimp ship moored out in the deeper water, inside the bar, from which it swung inland again, and, as I watched it a good five minutes, kept turning more and more to the west, into the sun, until that peculiar movement of the wings began to give way to the more usual flight of a chii-mi. And I figure, as it disappeared, it was all right, all right.

God, it was wonderful, black, wonderful long feathers, and the wing spread, overall, what, five to six feet. Never got such a sense of a bird's strength, inside strength, as this one gave, like I say, more animal, seemingly, and sure, none of that small beating heart. That's why its victory, over these mean little pricks, was so fine.

(Its silhouette, anyway, above us each day, is a lovely thing, the fore part of the wing not a curve as in a gull, but angled like a bat's a third out from the body. And this strange double tail splitting in flight like the steepest sort of an arrow.

How come 'chii-mi' I can't yet tell you, though, last night, in my Dictionario Motul, which arrived yesterday from Merida and gives me a fair start in to the ride of this Maya tongue, I was able to locate 'chii,' as 'margin' of the sea, a page, a dress, etcetera. 'Mi' I still can't find in the proliferation of double consonants, double vowels, and five extra letters beyond Western alphabets (I daresay if I had Tozzer's Maya-English dictionary (the only one, I now learn), I'd be better off. To try to find anything through the screen of one unknown language to another! (this D. Motul is the base work, Maya-Espanol, done here in the Yucatan mid-16th century, and not equalled since. My edition is by the one Mexican scholar whom I have yet had occasion to raise respect for, a 82 yr old citizen named Juan Martínez Hernández.)...

But I've been happier, by an act of circumvention, the last three days: I have been in the field, away from people, working around stones in the sun, putting my hands in to the dust and fragments and pieces of those Maya who used to live here down and along this road.

And the joy is, the whole area within the easiest walking distances, is covered with their leavings: I already have in front of me as I write to you the upper half of an owl idol's (?) head, which I picked up on a farm five minutes from the house! And two half plates, among other fragments of pots, quite fine in the working of the clay, though the painting is average.

The big thing, tho, is the solidity of the sense of their lives one can get right here in the fields and on the hill which rises quite steeply from the shore. Thursday afternoon Con and I went back in, say, five miles, and ran into something which would take the top off yr head: on the highest hill, looking out over a savannah which runs straight and flat to the sea here, a sort of farm moor (it was maize once, but, due to the way of Mayan agriculture, grass defeated corn inside of seven years, and from then on, the grass is so durable, neither forest nor corn can come again), on that hill where the sea's winds reach, where the overlook is so fine, these Maya had once built what appears to have been a little city. I say appears, for now, after six years of the Sanchez Construction Co. crushing the stones of that city, we were able to see only one piece of one column of what (the Indian workers told us) was once, six years ago, many many such columns *in place!* (The whole experience was like the deserts we found in and around Sacramento, where the gold Companies have, with their huge water shitting machines, spoiled the earth (in this case not men's work, but nature's soil accumulation, for ever, mind you, forever: they turn the top soil down under and pile on top of it as their crawling machine goes along, all the crunched gravel and stone their water-test has proven not to contain gold, or the dust, of gold)

Crazy, 'stupido,' as the Indians at least, know it to be: it angers me two ways (1) that the rubble beneath the facings, columns, worked facades, etc., is the bulk of the stone and there is no reason except laziness, that the worked things, so small a part of the whole, should not have been set aside; and (2) that this is the laziness, not of Sanchez & Co., which one has to grant its stupidity, but is the stupidity & laziness of the archaeologists, both American & Mexican, which is that most culpable of all, intellectual carelessness.

I had the feeling, already in Merida, that the Peabody-Carnegie gang, whatever they may have done, 50, or 25 years ago, were, now, missing the job, were typical pedants or academics, and were playing some state & low professional game. Like this: that, at this date, it was no longer so important to uncover buried cities and restore same, as it was to strike in anew by two paths: (1) what I have already sounded off to you about, the living Maya language and what its perdurables, because language is so tough, may well contain in the heads of these living farmers back one block, from this street, or wherever, the deeper in, I imagine, the more and (2) in the present context the important one: a total reconnaissance of *all* sites (laugh as they did at me in Merida, the 'experts') instead of (as the Carnegie-Mexican Govt is about to launch) the recovery of the 3rd of the Maya Metropolises here in the peninsula, Mayapan.

The joker is, they are 'advanced' enough to justify the Mayapan operation as a step to discover more abt the economic & political life of the ancient Maya! Which, of course, kills me. Here I am an aestheticist (which I have yet to be convinced *any* one of them, from Stephens on down, is). And now, when they, these professionals, are catching on (EP's 35 yr lag, surely), to the validity of the total life of a people as what cargo art discharges, I am the one who is arguing that the correct way to come to an estimate of that dense & total thing is not, again, to measure the walls of a huge city but to get down, before it is too late, on a flat thing called a map, as complete a survey as possible of all, all present ruins, small as most of them are.

They'll cry, these fat & supported characters: 'Oh, they are all over the place, these, ruins!' Which is quite, quite the big & astounding fact – so much so are they all over the place that Sanchez & Co., Campeche, Mex., is not the only sand & gravel company in business: already, in this walking area from this house, I have come to learn of four sites – and of some size more than 'small' – which have been already reduced to white cement in bags! (That it has taken Sanchez six years of daily grinding at the site – no where, by the way, listed as a site – the natives here in Lerma call it Casa Vieja – to take only the face off the city, may be a gauge of ((what I had no way of knowing, in Merida)) the extent of these ignored, or smiled at, spots where, 1500 years ago, for, o, say, 500 years, a people went about human business...

tues. (carlos, the letter carrier, abt due / sort of the village idiot, i take it: walks like no fisherman, smiles like a gringo, and is altogether not native, is 'allegre,' slap-happy, and of whom I am most fond: yesterday, bringing yr letter, he holds out two us air mail sts (enclosed)! I say, how come, and, as I understood, he had noticed that, they had not been cancelled. So he had carefully removed them from the envelopes, and brought them to me! So here they are, for you.

You will imagine, knowing my bias toward just such close use of things, how much all these people make sense to me (coca-cola tops are the boys' tiddley-winks; the valves of bicycle tubes, are toy guns; bottles are used and re-used, even sold, as cans are; old tires are the base foot-wear of this whole peninsula (the modern Maya sandal is, rope plus Goodyear); light is candle or kerosene, and one light to a house, even when it is a foco, for electricidad

and last night, at the store, for a beer, after they had closed, got into one of those conversations one does, with storekeepers, when they are sloping off: the wife was pinching off 8 peppercorns per packet of newspaper (5 centavos) / the page was open to a television ad (Mexico City) / they both ask me / I say MALO, MAS MALO QUE RADIO / but then, sez the husband, the straight and surest question imaginable (Newsreel Companies please note, as well as the Dept of Disappearing Culture) – POSSIBLE TO SEE LA GUERRA?

by god, that kills me: Con tells me a kid on the beach went straight to the same, 1st question, too: possi-ble, to see, la GUERRA?...

                lerma march 8

Yr letter! How it spotted itself. This way: (1) arrived precise to eclipse of sun (1/2); (2) arrived at climax of long gab with Con in which... I had made this proposition: that Kukulkan vs the Chichimee was the true contest, not the Spanish, and that I proposed to pick up again, now here, on the life of this very great man, saying to Con, that, with so much registration of him in codices, frescoes, stone cutting, stucco, it should be as possible, or more, to recreate him as, that Barlow, from mss., sought to do same by Montezuma:

    had just sd, 'I forgot to tell you, that, at Champoton, after you took the bus last Sunday, I got into conversation with a bar boy, there, and, talking abt the Isla Cuyo (the remnant now standing in the sea of the pyramid K had erected for himself, there, on departing Tula-ward, he having done his work, here), it was my notion, that, that he had the imagination to build *in the sea,* was another sign of how unique he was' (asking myself, the relation of same act to (1) the fact that the Maya hereabouts put their cities (in contrast to all since) on the hill over the sea ('Señor gusta monte,' sd the lady, fr whom, bananas, on the road in, one day), (2) the Island of Jaina, just above us here, abt as far north of us as Champoton is south, and not yet visited because it *has* to be *reached by sea* (had most beautiful workmen in clay), and (3) that, on the east coast, the big beautiful place is TULUM, and, the *Island* of Cozumel (by map in yesterday fr Tulane, the sites on Cozumel are thick ((propose to go there, if possible to swing it: three days by sailing vessel from Progreso))

when LETTER-LIGHT, comes in the midst of a context unduplicatable – (1) the stir outside with all, *all,* kids & grown ups, watching, the eclipsa, excited (contrast to States, abt 1930, when, a total eclipse, and only me and the birds, apparently, aware, until it was suddenly dark) here, with no real shrinkage of light, yet, everyone, these descendants of astronomers, than whom none more effective than one Kukulkan, apparently ((the month CEH, as, I believe, in last letter I identified as HIS new fire ceremony – Spinden dates its institution as 1168 with a Day 1 Knife, when K started a year count as Year 1 Knife, and in Year 2 Reed, 1194-5, he declared the Fire Ceremony to be celebrated at intervals of 52 years)) all of them, with smoked glass and old film and rolled up newspapers, anything, looking, upward; (2) the conversation, me still beating around, these things
                                                                                                           &

(3) CARLOS WALKS IN WITH YR NEWS, YR NEWS, BRO, OF K & a sea-horse (for same thing, a sea-horse, is also precise: using as fetish to hold down yr letters in the wind which sweeps through this room, what do I have, have had since third day after arrival, as present from a boy I have never seen since? and same thing I have thought again & again, it's light, and I should like to send it to you & Ann & kids as SIGN, but haven't because, to box something seems beyond huge, for to get a letter off, a money order say, is already proved murder: one for book fr Merida lost already!

And now it is too late. For you have it, already. And have made me the present! Beautiful. And tell Slater, for me, he's HOT. Or so I'd guess, round abt now, with, what is in hand:

Let me go back.

I: why I still beat up against this biz of, getting rid of nomination, so that historical material is free for forms now, is

> Ez's epic solves problem by his ego: his single emotion breaks all down to his equals or inferiors (so far as I can see only two, possibly, are admitted, by him, to be his betters – Confucius, & Dante. Which assumption, that there are intelligent men whom he can outtalk, is beautiful because it destroys historical time, and

> thus creates the methodology of the Cantos, viz, a space-field where, by inversion, though the material is all time material, he has driven through it so sharply by the beak of his ego, that, he has turned time into what we must now have, space & its live air

>> ((secondary contrast is Joyce, who, it comes to me now, did not improve on Duns Scotus Erigenus, or the Irish of the time the Irish were the culture-bosses, what was it, 7th-9th century, or something: he tried to get at the problem by running one language into another so as to create a universal language of the unconscious. Which is, finally, mush & shit, that is, now. Not so, then, DSE or Irishers, for then Europe was, both in language & dream, of that order.

>>> (((further thot: Joyce, the Commercial Traveller: the worship of IARichards – by the same people, accurately enough, who mug Joyce – is more honest: that is, that this internationalizing of language is more relevant to commerce, now, than it is to the aesthetic problem.
>>>> ((((all this a better way to say, he, ENDER)

> the primary contrast, for our purposes is, BILL: his Pat is exact opposite of Ez's, that is, Bill HAS an emotional system which is capable of extensions & comprehensions the ego-system (the Old Deal, Ez as Cento Man, here dates) is not. Yet

VI. OUTSIDE THE BOX

by making his substance historical of one city (the Joyce deal), Bill completely licks himself, lets time roll him under as Ez does not, and thus, so far as what is the more important, methodology, contributes nothing, in fact, delays, deters, and hampers, by not having busted through the very problem which Ez has so brilliantly faced, & beat

Which ought to – if my mouth had words in it, this morning – bring you to see why I hammer, on, nomination, thus:
            each of the above jobs are HALVES, that is, I take it (1) that the EGO AS BEAK is bent and busted but (2) whatever it is that we can call its replacement (Bill very much a little of it) HAS, SO FAR, not been able to bring any time so abreast of us that we are in this present air, going straight out, of our selves, into it

You see, I followed you, a bit back, when, in responding on Tarot & Maya, you sd, sure, & it's whatever you or anyone makes hot, is hot. Of course.

& two: that, we already have both (1) the ego as responsible to more than itself and (2) absolute clarity, that, time, is done, as effect of work in hand

Perhaps, as I sd before, I am only arguing with myself, that is, I am trying to see how to throw the materials I am interested in so that they take, with all impact of a correct methodology AND WITH THE ALTERNATIVE TO THE EGO-POSITION

I keep thinking, it comes to this: culture displacing the state. Which is my guess as to why Ez sounds so flat, when, he is just talking, when, he is outside the Cantos, say, that walker of his, than which there is, yet, no better
 (so much of Ez is, the 19th century stance:
  PROTEST, (Dahlberg is the funny man, of same biz: they both wld
    love to have been, who was it, Lousie 14th, 'l'état, c'est
    moi'?
    what burns me, is, they never speak, in their slash at the
    State or the Economy, basically, for anyone but
    themselves. And thus, it is Bohemianism

    and much too late, just abt as late as before Fourier,
    Marx, & Nietzsche, not to mention the real guys, then,
    Riemann or any of the geometers who were really
    cutting ahead

Tho, again, here, one has to give Ez his due: that he did write
KULCH

Which ought to get us to II, or, Kukulkan. This way:
why the problem is tougher than Ez's throw, or Bill's failure, is that, the shift is SUBSTANTIVE (it delights me, to recognize, that, the word has that other meaning, of 'noun'!)
that is, another reason why i don't think Ez's toucan works after 1917 is, that, after that date, the materials of history which he has found useful are not at all of use (nor are Bill's, despite the more apparent homogeneity: date 1917, not only did Yurrup (West, Cento, Renaissance) go, but such blueberry America as Bill presents (Jersey dump-smoke covering same) also WENT (that is, Bill, with all respect, don't know fr nothing abt what a city *is*)
the which says this: that the substances of history now useful lie outside, under, right here, anywhere but in the direct continuum of society as we have had it (of the State, same, of the Economy, same, of the Politicks: Ez is traitor as Dante was, to Florence: the difference of F to USA is not difference at all, other than, the passage of time & time's dreary accumulations by repetition

(((something of this must have been what Razl meant, when he sd, HISTORY IS UNIVERSAL MONOTONY)))

(*Note:* I note that I assume history is prime, even now. I assume it is. I assume this one thing – man's curiosity abt what his brother zopalotes have been about – comes through to us straight from that previous civilization, and is the one thread we better damn well hang on to. And the only one.

Perhaps because it is as much prime, as, an eclipse?

The substance has changed. Period. BUT: we are confronted, as men forever are, by the LAG. Our fellow cits are, I take it, quite easily thrown off by any noun which contains Z's and X's. (Not, again, that, thus superficially, it matters a good god damn: bust them over the heads. Right. Only, what i am saying is, that, to use X's and Z's makes for the difficulties John Adams, or Kung Fu Sze, or even Omeros, don't. ((Or is this just a little bit argumentative, & petulant, as one is, when the work is not done, and one is talking abt it instead.))

((Doesn't matter. For, as you'd guess, the operation is otherwise, is, actually, the other edge: how *was* this Kukulkan, how are you, Mister C)))

How can I pick up these injuns – that is, as Stephens, Prescott, Parkman did not so pick them up 100 yr agone, that, at the same moment of time as one H. Melville, they made them stick as he did, Pacifica? What's wrong – or, likewise, Sumeria. Or mao. Or usa, today.

NO. Erase the above. Somewhere I've been dragged off the methodological, here, by my own mention of the substantive. And am sucked into a substantive argument. Which is not what we're here for. Let me try it another way. For it's still this man Kukulkan we are talking abt.

Shots:

(1) are not the Maya the most important characters in the whole panorama (diorama was the word contemporary to above fine 4 workers) simply because the TOP CLASS in their society, the bosses, were a class whose daily business was KNOWLEDGE, & its OFF-SHOOT, culture?

that thus a man of K's temper & interest could become Big Boss, & then, God?

and that any such society goes down easily before a gun? or bows & arrows, when Chichemecs come along with same? ((The absolute quote here, is, one prime devil, Goebbels, who sd: 'When I hear the word 'kultur' I reach for my gun.'))

(2) that such a society is precisely the contrary (really the contrary, not the opposite, to use Blake's careful discrimination, and, by so doing, show up the collective or communist deal for what it is, and will continue to be as long as the rest of the world wants what America has had

Comes up, out of the sea, a sea
horse (my question is, where
here
do the rains

come from, is the serpent
who shall fight the jaguar
another norther, of
another season, is
weather, here, as on the earth because
the earth turns eastward, is
all movements, as was the people's coming, is it from
the west?

they say
he was the wind, they say
also rain, anyway
he was water, not
sun fire not this heat which makes the day less
than the night

he wore a hat, a sort of silly hat, had
short breeches, a tortoise back with mirror on it, and
a tail: he died
just as the heat was at its worst, just
on the day the fields were burnt, just that day the morning
star rose anew

      his eyes, she sd,
      were like a caracol. And when he left us, he
      walked straight out into the sea, west
         he was also
         a bachelor
            but what
seemed most important, he
was just, was
a child
of water, they figured it, was
precisely what
they needed, was
the image of
(Well! To hell with that. Pardon me. Get up off my face, olson.)
themselves.

It is a beautiful thing, what Slater found. You are right, of course: it bears
right in on what I have been turning over.

what i can't find anything out about, is WATER. Judging from the bizness here now – and adding it to the *apparent* fact that the Maya depended, for water, upon these accidents of nature, where the upper limestone crust collapsed, and created these huge cenotes, near which they built their cities – I'd guess that this people had a very ancient way of *not improving on nature*, that is, that it is not a question of either intelligence or spirituality, but another thing, something Americans have a hard time getting their minds around, a form or bias of attention which does not include *improvements*

AND (by that law of the toilet, beds, etc., I wrote you about once, from Washington – how I can never worry) I'm not one myself to say they were *backward*, *are* backward (my god, talk about the stars here: I ought to get off to you about the *flesh* here! Jesus, to ride a bus with these people, of a Sunday, down the coast, the stopping, the variation of quality between, say, Seybaplaya (allegre) and La Jolla (a sugar cane plant there, and a bottom, all, creatures, most of them, garage proletariat – to steal, an accurate, phrase)

BUT, the way the bulk of them still (the 'unimproved') wear their flesh! It is something I never had the occasion to guess, except in small pieces, isolated moments like, say, an Eyetalian family, or some splinter, not making itself clear enough to take over my assurances. For this is very much the result, I'd take it, as, the agriculture, the water problem: the flesh is worn as a daily thing, like the sun, is – & only in this sense – a common, carried as the other things are, for use. And not at all exclusively sexual, as, it strikes me, the flesh is hardened, and like wires, focused ('foco' is the name for an electric light bulb, here) in the industrial States. The result (and this is what I think is actually the way to put what Slater makes spiritual or sacred) is, that the individual peering out from that flesh is precisely himself, is, a curious wandering animal (it is so very beautiful, how animal the eyes are, when the flesh is not worn so close it chokes, how human and individuated the look comes out: jeesus, when you are rocked, by the roads, against any of them – kids, women, men – it's so very gentle, so granted, the feel, of touch – none of that pull, away, which, in the States caused me, for so many years, the deepest sort of questions about my own structure, the complex of my own organism, I felt so very much this admission these people now give me

This is not easy to state, I guess. BUT OF EXTREME IMPORTANCE. For I come on, here, what seems to me the real, live clue to the results of what I keep gabbing about, *another* humanism. For it is so much a matter of resistance – like I tried to say, about, *leaving* the difficulties, not removing them, by *buying* the improvements so readily available at the corner. You buy something all right, but what gets forgotten is, that you sell, in that moment of buying – you sell a whole disposition of self which very soon plunders you just where you are not looking. Or so, it seems.

                                                                                     The trouble is, with this imagery, of industrial man. I distrust it, as (1) too easy (2) too modern and (3) too much, not contrary, but merely oppositional. For the shift, which took away, (is taking away, so rapidly, that I shall soon not be able to get into Campeche, it is such an ugly ('feo,' is their word) demonstration of what happens when COMMERCE comes in) – how do you get at what happened? when did some contrary principle of man get in business? why? what urge

well, that's not hard, I know – i figure it always was, only, once (or still, here, at Seybaplaya – and a bit back, Lerma, before electricity) these big-eared, small-eyed, scared-flesh characters stayed as the minority, were not let out of, their holes. Because there was a concept at work, not surely 'sacred,' just a disposition to keep the attention poised in such a way that there was time to (1) be interested in expression & gesture of all creatures including at least three large planets enough to create a system of record which we now call hieroglyphs; (2) to mass stone with sufficient proportion to decorate a near hill and turn it into a firetower, or an observatory, or as one post of an enclosure in which people, favored by its shadows, might swap camotes for shoes; (3) to fire clay, not just to sift and thus make cool water, or, to stew iguana, or fish, but to fire it so that its handsomeness put ceremony where it also belongs, in the most elementary human acts. And when a people are so disposed, it should come as no surprise that, long before any of these accomplishments, the same people did an improvement, if one likes, of nature – the domestication of maize – which is still talked of as one of the world's wonders!

It is all such a delicate juggling of weights, this culture business – exactly like, I'd guess, what is the juggling of any one of us with the given insides. Which is why generalization is, a greased slide.

Christ, these hieroglyphs. Here is the most abstract and formal deal of all the things this people dealt out – and yet, to my taste, it is precisely as intimate as verse is. Is, in fact, verse. Is their verse. And comes into existence, obeys the same laws that, the coming into existence, the persisting of verse, does.

Which leads me to use again Ruth Benedict's excellent proposition (to counter the notion that, the Maya, having done so much, need also have developed an agronomy which would not have exhausted their soil and a system of rain-gathering which would also have licked the thirst problem): says Benedict

> ... techniques of cultural change which are limited only by the *unimaginativeness of the human mind*

Or which, perhaps, is just a little bit the bitterness of an old-maid almost-Communist before she died. It seems to me now, she over-loads, by using 'imagination,' even negatively – a little bit too much modern Hamletism (I am thinking of Hamlet to Horatio (is it) on what a glory man is, the top creature, what nature, was working toward, etc.) Benedict is still the reverse of same. One needs to be quieter – but still not miss the point: that, in a given lifetime a man, or, in a given expression, a culture cannot get any more done than it can get done: that time, & our life-machine, are not infinitely extensible. Which dream – the Renaissance, & all ecstatic propositions – is well dead. We'll know more and do more if the limits – there'll be more reaches, etc.

My point is, what more do we have the privilege to ask of the Maya than same Maya offered...

sunday   april 1

... What continues to hold me, is, the tremendous levy on all objects as they present themselves to human sense, in this glyph-world. And the proportion, the distribution of weight given same parts of all, seems, exceptionally, distributed & accurate, that is, that

>   sun
>   moon
>   venus
>   other constellations & zodiac
>   snakes
>   ticks
>   vultures

    jaguar
        owl
            frog
  feathers
      peyote
           water-lily
not to speak of
fish
    caracol
        tortoise

&, above all,
human eyes
    hands
        limbs   (PLUS EXCEEDINGLY CAREFUL OBSERVATION OF ALL POSSIBLE INTERVALS OF SAME, as well as ALL ABOVE (to precise dimension of eclipses, say, & time of, same etc. etc.)

And the weights of same, each to the other, is, immaculate (as well as, full)

That is, the gate to the center was, here, as accurate as what you & i have been (all along) talking about – viz., man as object in field of force declaring self as force because is force in exactly such relation & can accomplish expression of self as force by conjecture, & displacement in a context best, now, seen as space more than a time such;   which, I take it, is precise contrary to, what we have had, as 'humanism,' with, man, out of all proportion of, relations, thus, so mis-centered, becomes, dependent on, only, a whole series of 'human' references which, so made make only anthropomorphism, and thus, make mush of, *any* reality, conspicuously, his own, not to speak of, how all other forces (ticks, water-lilies, or snails) become only descriptive objects in what used to go with antimacassars, those, planetariums (ancestors of gold-fish bowls) etc.

This gate got to, gone in by, 2nd stage, follows, that is, *invention* produces narration & verse also of a contrary order (the last example of which, which comes down to us, being,

ODYSSEY

which, for my dough, is not good enough (ditto only modern example i know, one melville) simply because humanism is (homer) coming in, and (melville) going out

and i take it, a Sumer poem or Maya glyph is more pertinent to our purposes than anything else, because each of these people & their workers had forms which unfolded directly from content (sd content itself a disposition toward reality which understood man as only force in field of force containing multiple other expressions

one delightful fact, just picked up: that *all* Mayan jobs (sez Tatiana Proskouriakoff) are built around *a single human figure*, in all reliefs, etc.

which is, of course, that ego which you, me, Mayan X were (are), he who is interested enough to, seeing it all, get something down

What has to be battered down, completely, is, that this has anything to do with stage of development. Au contraire. The capacity for (1) the observation & (2) the invention has no more to do with brick or no wheels or metal or stone than you and i are different from, sd peoples: we are like. Therefore, there is no 'history.' (I still keep going back to, the notion, this is (we are) merely, the *second time* (that's as much history as I'll permit in, which ain't history at all: seems so, only, because we have been all dragooned into a notion that, what came between was, better. Which is eatable shit, for the likes of those who like, same.

Animation of what presents itself, fr the thing on outwards: rock as vessel, vessel as tale, creating, men & women, because narrator and/or poet happen to be man or woman, thus, human figure as part of universe of things...

To Gerhardt, There, Among Europe's Things of which He Has Written Us in His 'Brief an Creeley und Olson'

The Proceedings of the Twenty-third International Congress of Americanists *(1930) was a forbiddingly weighty volume to pack for Mexico. Olson took it for the Mayan material, but the end result was this poem. The 'nerve' running through the verse on the right side of the page (with 'o Old Man' and after) was all from N.P. Dyrenkova's contribution, 'Bear Worship Among Turkish Tribes of Siberia' (pp. 411–40). A letter from Rainer Gerhardt had triggered afresh Olson's antipathy to the 'box' of Western culture, an aversion that was concurrently finding its formal expression in the 'Human Universe' essay and the attempt there to find an 'alternative to the whole Greek system'. Rhys Carpenter's* Folk Tale, Fiction, Saga in Homeric Epics *(1946) had convinced Olson that the old Bear-son folktale lay behind Odysseus. Therefore, Northern mythology would be the back door of his inheritance that Gerhardt ('this long last Bear-son') should take in order to liberate himself from the influence, demonstrated in his* brief, *of St-John Perse, Eliot, Pound (who snorted 'bric-a-brac' and 'did not know whereof he spoke'), and even the false, if superb, dimension of Dante. This epistolary poem is Olson, in the first act of the archaic post-modern, giving Gerhardt 'a present': the present that is* prologue, der Weg.

so pawed,
by this long last Bear-son

      with no crockery broken,
      but no smile in my mouth

            June 28th, '51, on this horst
            on the Heat Equator, a mediterranean sea
            to the east, and north
            what saves America from desert, waters
            and thus rain-bearing winds,
            by subsidence, salt-waters
            (by which they came,
            the whelps, looking
            for youth

VI. OUTSIDE THE BOX

Which they found.
                And have continuously sought
                              to kill

        (o Old Man,

            in winter, when before me, cross my path

            in summer, when behind me, cross my path

    If you want to shut yourself in, shut yourself in
    If you do not want to shut yourself in, come out

                A zoo
                is what he's come to, the old
                Beginner, the old
                Winner

Who took all,
for awhile

            (My grandfather, my grandmother,
            why have you died?
            Did a hand to hand struggle come?
            Did a war, the size of a man's fist come?)

1
The proposition, Gerhardt
is to get it straight, right
from the start.

            Help raise the bones
            of the great man.

            Meat and bones we won't throw away,
            We pile it up in a lonely place.

            We do not throw on the ground.
            Your meat and bones without purpose.
            We take bones and meat.

            O Grandfather,
            you went to war

The first duty is
to knock out his teeth, saying
'These are the teeth with which you devour all animals.'

I offer you no proper names
either from great cities
on the other side of civilization
which have only to be visited
to be got the hell out of, by bus
or motorcycle, simply because place
as a force is a lie,
or at most a small truth,
now that man has no oar to screw down into the earth, and say
here i'll plant, does not know
why he should cease
staying on the prowl

        You climbed up the tree after some foul berry
        and fell down and died
        You ate berries, fell from the rock
        and died
        You ate sorb berries
        and died
        You ate raspberries,
        drowned in the swamp and died

Or from the other side of time, from a time on the other side of yourself
from which you have so lightly borrowed men, naming them as though,
like your litany of Europe's places, you could take up
their power: magic, my light-fingered faust,
is not so easily sympathetic. Nor are the ladies
worn so decoratively.

        The top of the spring plant
        noisily chewing

        The top of the summer plant
        noisily chewing

        On a summer day walk before and behind me
        on a winter day

2
Nor can I talk of method, in the face of your letter,
in verse or otherwise,
as though it were a dance
of rains, or schmerz, of words as signs worn
like a toupee on the head of a Poe cast
in plaster, any method otherwise than
he practised it who gave it up,
after a summer in his mother's barn,
because the place smelled so, because time
his time, precisely this now
And with no back references, no
floating over Asia arrogating
how a raiding party moves in advance of a nation, thereby eventually
giving a language the international power
poets take advantage of. As they also,
with much less reason, from too much economics speak
of the dream
in a peasant's bent shoulders, as though it were true
they cared a damn
for his conversation

> On a mountain with dry stalks, walk
> with a resounding tread
>
> On a mountain with meadow-sweet
> walk with a resounding tread
>
> On the way to your fathers,
> join them

3
Not of a film, or of strange birds,
or of ordinary ones. Nor with the power of American vocables
would I arm you in Kansas, when you come,
or there, if you have to stay, where you feel so strongly
the dead center of the top of time

> I am giving you a present
>
> I am giving you a present

For you forget (forgetting
is much more your problem
than you know, right-handed one
who so beautifully reminds me
that the birds stand
in the middle of the air
and that always, in that apsed place
in which so many have kneeled
as I do not have the soul to kneel, the fields
are forever harvested, and happy heaven
leans over backwards
to pour its blessings by downfall
on to black earth

Admitting that among the ruins
      with a like schmerz in every vessel of his throat,
      he repeated, 'Among the ruins, among them
      the finest memory in the Orient'
one will go about picking up old pieces
      bric-a-brac, he snorted, who did not know whereof he spoke,
      he had so allowed himself to be removed, to back-trail
or put it immediately out of the mind, as some can,
stuff the construction hole quickly with a skyscraper

but you will remember that even Caesar comes to this, certainly you
who has written of Hamlet's death, who is able to handle such large counters
as the classic poet handled bank-notes in our time, before prizes
were his lot, and I am envious, who can do neither

that the point of the rotting of man in his place is also
(beside the long-lived earth of good farmers, its manuring,
what Duncan pointed out America and Russia are very careless with)
what blows about and blocks a hole where the wind was used to go

              (While walking on the earth with stalks
              you received a present

              While walking on the earth with the stalks of plants
              your head was crushed

              You could not see, your eyes got small,
              you could not defecate, you were small
              you could not,
              therefore you died

VI. OUTSIDE THE BOX

It is a rod of mountain ash I give you, Rainer Maria Gerhardt,
instead of any other thing, in order that you may also be
left-handed, as he was, your Grandfather,
whom you have all forgotten, have even lost the song of, how
he was to be addressed:
> 'Great man,
> in climbing up the tree,
> broke his leg.'

I am urging you from here
where nothing is brutal,
not even the old economics
   (I do not dare to breathe
   for what I know the new
   will do) and only the kids kill
frigate-birds, because they have to
to develop a throwing arm

> (as your people knew, if I can lead you
> to go back far enough,
> which is not one step from where you are

> 'His ear is the earth.
> Let you be careful'

> that he must be hunted, that to eat
> you shall bring him down

> 'Your head
> is the size of a ladle

> Your soul
> is of the size of a thread

> Do not enter my soul by day,
> do not enter my dreams by night

> that woman – who is, with more resistance
> than you seem to have allowed, named –
> lends herself to him as concubine

what you forget is, you

are their son! You are not

Telemachus. And that you come back

under your own

steam

There are no broken stones, no statues, no images, phrases, composition
otherwise than
what Creeley and I also have,
and without reference to
what reigned in the house
and is now well dismissed

Let you pray to him, we say
who are without such fatherhood:

    'Show your house in spring.

    Show a mound of snow in your house in winter.

    In summer go in back of and in front
    of the children.

    Think not badly of the man, go right.'

4
Or come here
where we will welcome you
with nothing but what is, with
no useful allusions, with no birds
but those we stone, nothing to eat
but ourselves, no end and no beginning, I assure you, yet
not at all primitive, living as we do in a space we do not need to contrive

And with predecessors who, though they are not our nouns, the verbs
are like!

So we are possessed of what you cry over, time
and magic numbers

    Language,
    my enemie,
    is no such system:

VI. OUTSIDE THE BOX

> 'Hey, old man, the war arrived.
>
> Be still, old man.
>
> Your mouth is shut,
> your door is shut,'

As I said, I am giving you a present.
To all false dimensions,
including his superb one
who refused to allow the social question in,
to all such fathers and false girls
(one of his, I notice, you take, seriously)
why not say what, somewhere, you must hear the echo of?

> 'One eye
> sees heaven,
> another eye
> sees earth'

For the problem is one of focus, of the field as well as the point of
vision: you will solve your problem best
without displacement

> 'One ear
> hears heaven,
> another ear
> hears earth.'

In such simplicities I would have you address me,
another time

5

> The old man, my grandfather, died.
> The old woman, my grandmother, died.
> And now my father visits me, clothed
> in a face he never wore, with an odor
> I do not know as his, as his was meadow-sweet.
> He sits, grieving, that she should have worried,
> and I look up at him as he sits there
> and if I am his son, this man
> is from as far a place and time

>   as yours is, carries with him
>   the strangeness you and I will carry
>   for our sons, and for like reason,
>   that we are such that can be pawed

>   'We are no murderers,' they used so carefully to say.

>   'We have put in order the bones of him
>   whom others kill.'

You see, we are experienced of what you speak of: silence
with no covering of ashes, geraniums also
and loaded with aphis

>   of all but war,

but war, too, is dead as the lotus is dead

>   And our hardness
has been exaggerated. You see,
we see nothing downward: we walk, as your grandfather walked,
without looking at his feet

>   'And because of meeting the great man,
>   a feast is held

>   Warm yourself,
>   over the fire of grandfather

>   This is an offering to the guests, a holiday
>   of the great man

>   He will feel satisfied

>   He will not take revenge

The stick is a reminder, Gerhardt. And the song? what seems
to have been forgotten?

Here it is (as we say here, in our anti-cultural speech, made up
of particulars only, which we don't, somehow, confuse with gossip:

VI. OUTSIDE THE BOX

'To his resting place in spring,

to his house in autumn,

I shall go

With autumn plant, arouse the mountain

With spring plant, arouse the mountain

In summer, walk in the background,
do not frighten the children,
do not sniff, neither here
nor there.'

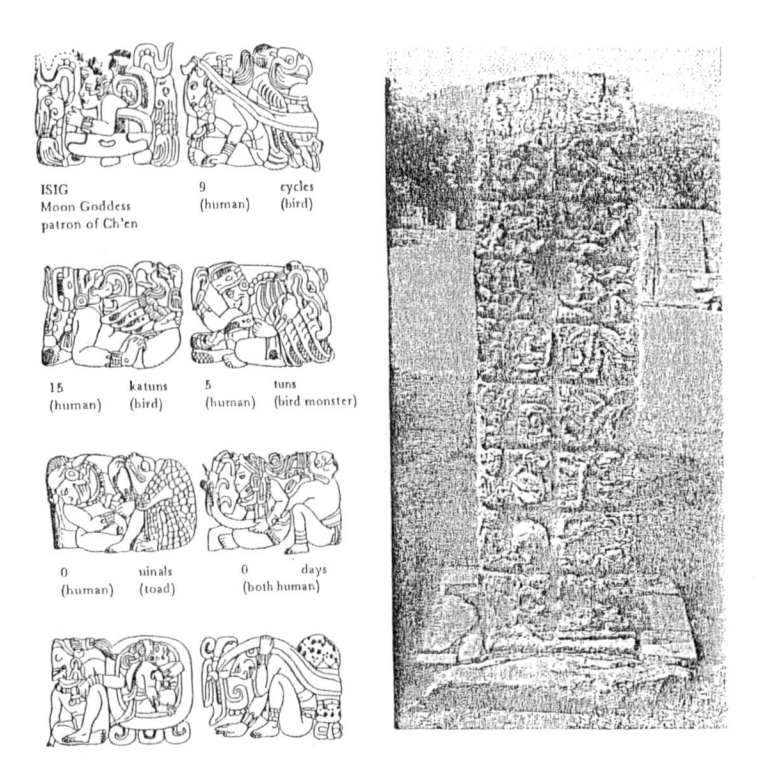

Figures from Stela D, Copan, Yucatan. The zopalote (vulture) can be seen in the top right-hand drawing. It represents a period of time equal to 144,000 days, and is carried by the human-figured glyph for the number 9. The full count for the glyph is 9 x 144,000 = 1,296,000 days. The figures 'carried' on the right-hand side of each glyph represent different time periods, hence the 'mass and weight' Olson says the Maya ascribed to time.

Human Universe

Out of his six months in the Yucatan Olson sacrificed a whole month to an application for a grant that might enable him to stay on. It annoyed him to have to use the 'grantese' expected of him when his proposal was to explore the poetry of hieroglyphs, a totally different kind of discourse. (It riled him further when he discovered he was in a classification that denied him a grant until he found 'institutional affiliation'.) 'I am most impatient with argument and logic,' Olson wrote to Cid Corman on 18 May 1951 in the midst of his grant application, 'not because I do not believe in same – in fact I trained myself from age of 14 on, in just such [and] to this very day I have not broken beyond' (CO/CC, p. 157). When he turned from the application to write the first words of the 'Human Universe' essay, 'There are laws', he was taking on something only just not beyond him, something that the Yucatan moment is beginning to make clear, a new mode of discourse. Since myth is at the root of the kind of cohesion that is being envisioned, the expository preamble of the essay appropriately merges into a folktale (from J.E.S. Thompson's Maya Hieroglyphic Writing *[1950]). Of the finished 'Human Universe,' Olson said to his friend, 'I have here set my cultural position, the body, the substance of my faith' (CO/CC, p. 183).*

There are laws, that is to say, the human universe is as discoverable as that other. And as definable.

The trouble has been, that a man stays so astonished he can triumph over his own incoherence, he settles for that, crows over it, and goes at a day again happy he at least makes a little sense. Or if he says anything to another, he thinks it is enough – the struggle does involve such labor and some terror – to wrap it in a little mystery: ah, the way is hard but this is what you find if you go it.

The need now is a cooler one, a discrimination, and then, a shout. Der Weg stirbt, sd one. And was right, was he not? Then the question is: was ist der Weg?

1

The difficulty of discovery (in the close world which the human is because it is ourselves and nothing outside us, like the other) is, that definition is as much a part of the act as is sensation itself, in this sense, that life *is* preoccupation with itself, that conjecture about it is as much of it as its coming at us, its going on. In other words, we are ourselves both the instrument of discovery and the instrument of definition.

Which is of course, why language is a prime of the matter and why, if we are to see some of the laws afresh, it is necessary to examine, first, the present condition of the language – and I mean language exactly in its double sense of discrimination (logos) and of shout (tongue).

We have lived long in a generalizing time, at least since 450 BC. And it has had its effects on the best of men, on the best of things. Logos, or discourse, for example, has, in that time, so worked its abstractions into our concept and use of language that language's other function, speech, seems so in need of restoration that several of us go back to hieroglyphs or to ideograms to right the balance. (The distinction here is between language as the act of the instant and language as the act of thought about the instant.)

But one can't any longer, stop there, if one ever could. For the habits of thought are the habits of action, and here, too, particularism has to be fought for, anew. In fact, by the very law of the identity of definition and discovery, who can extricate language from action? (Though it is one of the first false faces of the law which I shall want to try to strike away, it is quite understandable – in the light of this identity – that the Greeks went on to declare all speculation as enclosed in the 'UNIVERSE of discourse'. It is their word, and the refuge of all metaphysicians since – as though language, too, was an absolute, instead of (as even man is) instrument, and not to be extended, however much the urge, to cover what each, man and language, is in the hands of: what we share, and which is enough, of power and of beauty, not to need an exaggeration of words, especially that spreading one, 'universe'. For discourse is hardly such, or at least only arbitrarily a universe. In any case, so extended (logos given so much more of its part than live speech), discourse has arrogated to itself a good deal of experience which needed to stay put – needs now to be returned to the only two universes which count, the two phenomenal ones, the two a man has need to bear on because they bear so on him: that of himself, as organism, and that of his environment, the earth and planets.

We stay unaware how two means of discourse the Greeks appear to have invented hugely intermit our participation in our experience, and so prevent discovery. They are what followed from Socrates' readiness to generalize, his willingness (from his own bias) to make a 'universe' out of discourse instead of letting it rest in its most serviceable place. (It is not sufficiently observed that logos, and the reason necessary to it, are only a stage which a man must master and not what they are taken to be, final discipline. Beyond them is direct perception and the contraries which dispose of argument. The harmony of the universe, and I include man, is not logical, or better, is post-logical, as is the order of any created thing.) With Aristotle, the two great means appear: logic and classification. And it is they that have so fastened themselves on habits of thought that action is interfered with, absolutely interfered with, I should say.

Nor can I let the third of the great Greeks, Plato, go free – he who had more of a sort of latitude and style my tribe of men are apt to indulge him for. His world of Ideas, of forms as extricable from content, is as much and as dangerous an issue as are logic and classification, and they need to be seen as such if we are to get on to some alternative to the whole Greek system. Plato may be a honey-head, as Melville called him, but he is precisely that – treacherous to all ants, and where, increasingly, my contemporaries die, or drown the best of themselves. Idealisms of any sort, like logic and like classification, intervene at just the moment they become more than the means they are, are allowed to become ways as end instead of ways *to* end, END, which is never more than this instant, than you on this instant, than you, figuring it out, and acting, so. If there is any absolute, it is never more than this one, you, this instant, in action.

Which ought to get us on. What makes most acts – of living and of writing – unsatisfactory, is that the person and/or the writer satisfy themselves that they can only make a form (what they say or do, or a story, a poem, whatever) by selecting from the full content some face of it, or plane, some part. And at just this point, by just this act, they fall back on the dodges of discourse, and immediately, they lose me, I am no longer engaged, this is not what I know is the going-on (and of which going-on I, as well as they, want some illumination, and so, some pleasure). It comes out a demonstration, a separating out, an act of classification, and so, a stopping, and all that I know is, it is not there, it has turned false. For any of us, at any instant, are juxtaposed to any experience, even an overwhelming single one, on several more planes than the arbitrary and discursive which we inherit can declare.

It is not the Greeks I blame. What it comes to is ourselves, that we do not find ways to hew to experience as it is, in our definition and expression of it, in other words, find ways to stay in the human universe, and not be led to partition reality at any point, in any way. For this is just what we do do, this is the real issue of what has been, and the process, as it now asserts itself, can be exposed. It is the function, *comparison*, or, its bigger name, *symbology*. These are the false faces, too much seen, which hide and keep from use the active intellectual states, metaphor and performance. All that comparison ever does is set up a series of *reference* points: to compare is to take one thing and try to understand it by marking its similarities to or differences from another thing. Right here is the trouble, that each thing is not so much like or different from another thing (these likenesses and differences are apparent) but that such an analysis only accomplishes a *description*, does not come to grips with what really matters: that a thing, any thing, impinges on us by a more important fact, its self-existence, without reference to any other thing, in short, the very character of it which calls our attention to it, which wants us to know more about it, its particularity. This is what we are confronted by, not the thing's 'class', any hierarchy, of quality or quantity, but the thing itself, and its *relevance* to ourselves who are the experience of it (whatever it may mean to someone else, or whatever other relations it may have).

There must be a means of expression for this, a way which is not divisive as all the tag ends and upendings of the Greek way are. There must be a way which bears *in* instead of away, which meets head on what goes on each split second, a way which does not – in order to define – prevent, deter, distract, and so cease the act of, discovering.

I have been living for some time amongst a people who are more or less directly the descendants of a culture and a civilization which was a contrary of that which we have known and of which we are the natural children. The marked thing about them is, that it is only love and flesh which seems to carry any sign of their antecedence, that all the rest which was once a greatness different from our own has gone down before the poundings of our way. And, now, except as their bodies jostle in a bus, or as they disclose the depth and tenacity of love among each other inside a family, they are poor failures of the modern world, incompetent even to arrange that, in the month of June, when the rains have not come far enough forward to fill the wells, they have water to wash in or to drink. They have lost the capacity of their predecessors to do anything in common. But they do one thing no modern knows the secret of, however he is still by nature possessed of it: they wear their flesh with that difference which the understanding that it is common leads to. When I am rocked by the roads against any of them – kids, women, men – their flesh is most gentle, is granted, touch is in no sense anything but the natural law of flesh, there is none of that pull-away which, in the States, causes a man for all the years of his life the deepest sort of questioning of the rights of himself to the wild reachings of his own organism. The admission these people give me and one another is direct, and the individual who peers out from that flesh is precisely himself, is a curious wandering animal like me – it is so very beautiful how animal human eyes are when the flesh is not worn so close it chokes, how human and individuated the look comes out of a human eye when the house of it is not exaggerated.

This is not easy to save from subjectivism, to state so that you understand that this is not an observation but a first law to a restoration of the human house. For what is marked about these Lermeros with whom I live (by contrast, for example, to the people of the city nearby) is that, here, the big-eared, small-eyed creatures stay as the minority they must always have been before garages made them valuable and allowed them out of their holes to proliferate and overrun the earth. Nothing is accident, and man, no less than nature, does nothing without plan or the discipline to make plan fact. And if it is true that we now live in fear of our own house, and can easily trace the reason for it, it is also true that we can trace reasons why those who do not or did not so live found out how to do other than we.

My assumption is, that these contemporary Maya are what they are because once there was a concept at work which kept attention so poised that (1) men were able to stay so interested in the expression and gesture of all creatures, including at least three planets in addition to the human face, eyes and hands, that they invented a system of written record, now called hieroglyphs, which, on its very face, is verse, the signs were so clearly and densely chosen that, cut in stone, they retain the power of the objects of which they are the images; (2) to mass stone with sufficient proportion to decorate a near hill and turn it into a fire-tower or an observatory or one post of an enclosure in which people, favored by its shadows, might swap caymotes for sandals; and (3) to fire clay into pots porous enough to sieve and thus cool water, strong enough to stew iguana and fish, and handsome enough to put ceremony where it also belongs, in the most elementary human acts. And when a people are so disposed, it should come as no surprise that, long before any of these accomplishments, the same people did an improvement on nature – the domestication of maize – which remains one of the world's wonders, even to a nation of Burbanks, and that long after all their accomplishments, they still carry their bodies with some of the savor and the flavor that the bodies of the Americans are as missing in as is their irrigated lettuce and their green-picked refrigerator-ripened fruit. For the truth is, that the management of external nature so that none of its virtu is lost, in vegetables or in art, is as much a delicate juggling of her content as is the same juggling by any one of us of our own. And when men are not such jugglers, are not able to manage a means of expression the equal of their own or nature's intricacy, the flesh does choke. The notion of fun comes to displace work as what we are here for. Spectatorism crowds out participation as the condition of culture. And bonuses and prizes are the rewards of labor contrived by the monopolies of business and government to protect themselves from the advancement in position of able men or that old assertion of an inventive man, his own shop. All individual energy and ingenuity is bought off – at a suggestion box or the cinema. Passivity conquers all. Even war and peace die (to be displaced by world government?) and man reverts to only two of his components, inertia and gas.

It is easy to phrase, too easy, and we have had enough of bright description. To say that in America the goods are as the fruits, and the people as the goods, all glistening but tasteless, accomplishes nothing in itself, for the overwhelming fact is, that the rest of the world wants nothing but to be the same. Value is perishing from the earth because no one cares to fight down to it beneath the glowing surfaces so attractive to all. Der Weg stirbt.

II

Can one restate man in any way to repossess him of his dynamic? I don't know. But for myself a first answer lies in his systemic particulars. The trouble with the inherited formulations which have helped to destroy him (the notion of himself as the center of phenomenon by fiat or of god as the center and man as god's chief reflection) is that both set aside nature as an unadmitted or suppressed third party, a sort of Holy Ghost which was allowed in once to touch men's tongues and then, because the fire was too great, was immediately banished to some sort of half place in between god and the devil – who actually, of course, thereby became the most powerful agent of all. The result, we have been the witnesses of: discovering this discarded thing nature, science has run away with everything. Tapping her power, fingering her like a child, giving her again her place, but without somehow, remembering what truth there was in man's centering the use of anything, god, devil, or holy ghost, in himself, science has upset all balance and blown value, man's peculiar responsibility, to the winds.

If unselectedness is man's original condition (such is more accurate a word than that lovely riding thing, chaos, which sounds like what it is, the most huge generalization of all, obviously making it necessary for man to invent a bearded giant to shape it for him) but if likewise, selectiveness is just as originally the impulse by which he proceeds to do something about the unselectedness, then one is forced, is one not, to look for some instrumentation in man's given which makes selection possible. And it has gone so far, that is, science has, as to wonder if the fingertips, are not very knowing knots in their own rights, little brains (little photo-electric cells, I think they now call the skin) which, immediately, in responding to external stimuli, make decisions! It is a remarkable and usable idea. For it is man's first cause of wonder how rapid he is in his taking in of what he does experience.

But when you have said that, have you not done one of two things, either forever damned yourself by making the 'soul' mechanical (it has long been the soul which has softly stood as a word to cover man as a selecting internal reality posed dangerously in the midst of those externals which the word chaos generously covers like Williams' paint) or you have possibly committed a greater crime. You have allowed that external reality is more than merely the substance which man takes in. By making the threshold of reception so important and by putting the instrumentation of selection so far out from its traditional place (the greatest humanist of them all opened a sonnet, 'Poor soul, the centre of my sinful earth'), you have gone so far as to imply that the skin itself, the meeting edge of man and external reality, is where all that matters does happen, that man and external reality are so involved with one another that, for man's purposes, they had better be taken as one.

It is some such crime by which I am willing to hazard a guess at a way to restore to man some of his lost relevance. For this metaphor of the senses – of the literal speed of light by which a man absorbs, instant on instant, all that phenomenon presents to him – is a fair image as well, my experience tells me, of the ways of his inner energy, of the ways of those other things which are usually, for some reason, separated from the external pick-ups – his dreams, for example, his thoughts (to speak as the predecessors spoke), his desires, sins, hopes, fears, faiths, loves. I am not able to satisfy myself that these so-called inner things are so separable from the objects, persons, events which are the content of them and by which man represents or re-enacts them despite the suck of symbol which has increased and increased since the great Greeks first promoted the idea of a transcendent world of forms. What I do see is that each man does make his own special selection from the phenomenal field, and it is thus that we begin to speak of personality, however I remain unaware that this particular act of individuation is peculiar to man, observable as it is in individuals of other species of nature's making (it behooves man now not to separate himself too jauntily from any of nature's creatures).

Even if one does follow personality up, does take the problem further in to those areas of function which may seem more peculiarly human (at least are more peculiarly the concern of a humanist), I equally cannot satisfy myself of the gain in thinking that the process by which man transposes phenomenon to his use is any more extricable from reception than reception itself is from the world. What happens at the skin is more like than different from what happens within. The process of image (to be more exact about transposition than the 'soul' allows or than the analysts do with their tricky 'symbol-maker') cannot be understood by separation from the stuff it works on. Here again, as throughout experience, the law remains, form is not isolated from content. The error of all other metaphysic is descriptive, is the profound error that Heisenberg had the intelligence to admit in his principle that a thing can be measured in its mass only by arbitrarily assuming a stopping of its motion, or in its motion only by neglecting, for the moment of the measuring, its mass. And either way, you are failing to get what you are after – so far as a human being goes, his life. There is only one thing you can do about kinetic, reenact it. Which is why the man said, he who possesses rhythm possesses the universe. And why art is the only twin life has – its only valid metaphysic. Art does not seek to describe but to enact. And if man is once more to possess intent in his life, and to take up the responsibility implicit in his life, he has to comprehend his own process as intact, from outside, by way of his skin, in, and by his own powers of conversion, out again. For there is this other part of the motion which we call life to be examined anew, that thing we overlove, man's action, that tremendous discharge of force which we overlove when we love it for its own sake but which (when it is good) is the equal of all intake plus all transposing.

It deserves this word, that it is the equal of its cause only when it proceeds unbroken from the threshold of a man through him and back out again, without loss of quality, to the external world from which it came, whether that external world take the shape of another human being or of the several human beings hidden by the generalization 'society' or of things themselves. In other words, the proposition here is that man at his peril breaks the full circuit of object, image, action at any point. The meeting edge of man and the world is also his cutting edge. If man is active, it is exactly here where experience comes in that it is delivered back, and if he stays fresh at the coming in he will be fresh at his going out. If he does not, all that he does inside his house is stale, more and more stale as he is less and less acute at the door. And his door is where he is responsible to more than himself. Man does influence external reality, and it can be stated without recourse to the stupidities of mysticism (which appears to love a mystery as much outside as it does in). If man chooses to treat external reality any differently than as part of his own process, in other words as anything other than relevant to his own inner life, then he will (being such a froward thing, and bound to use his energy willy-nilly, nature is so subtle) use it otherwise. He will use it just exactly as he has used it now for too long, for arbitrary and willful purposes which, in their effects, not only change the face of nature but actually arrest and divert her force until man turns it even against herself, he is so powerful, this little thing. But what little willful modern man will not recognize is, that when he turns it against her he turns it against himself, held in the hand of nature as man forever is, to his use of himself if he choose, to his disuse, as he has.

What gets me is, how man refuses to acknowledge the consequences of his disposing of himself at his own entrance – as though a kiss were a cheap thing, as though he were. He will give a Rimbaud a lot of lip and no service at all, as though Rimbaud were a sport of nature and not a proof. Or a people different from himself – they will be the subject of historians' studies or of tourists' curiosity, and be let go at that, no matter how much they may disclose values he and his kind, you would think, could make use of. I have found, for example, that the hieroglyphs of the Maya disclose a placement of themselves toward nature of enormous contradiction to ourselves, and yet I am not aware that any of the possible usages of this difference have been allowed to seep out into present society. All that is done is what a Toynbee does, diminish the energy once here expended into the sieve phonetic words have become to be offered like one of nature's pastes that we call jewels to be hung as a decoration of knowledge upon some Christian and therefore eternal and holy neck. It is unbearable what knowledge of the past has been allowed to become, what function of human memory has been dribbled out to in the hands of these learned monsters whom people are led to think 'know'. They know nothing in not knowing how to reify what they do know. What is worse, they do not know how to pass over to us the energy implicit in any high work of the past because they purposely destroy that energy as dangerous to the States for which they work – which it is, for any concrete thing is a danger to rhetoricians and politicians, as dangerous as a hard coin is to a banker. And the more I live the more I am tempted to think that the ultimate reason why man departs from nature and thus departs from his own chance is that he is part of a herd which wants to do the very thing which nature disallows – that energy can be lost. When I look at the filth and lumber which man is led by, I see man's greatest achievement in this childish accomplishment – that he damn well can, and does, destroy destroy destroy energy every day. It is too much. It is too much to waste time on, this idiot who spills his fluids like some truculent and fingerless chamaco hereabouts who wastes water at the pump when birds are dying all over the country in this hottest of the months and women come in droves in the morning begging for even a tasa of the precious stuff to be poured in the amphoras they swing on their hips as they swing their babies. Man has made himself an ugliness and a bore.

It was better to be a bird, as these Maya seem to have been, they kept moving their heads so nervously to stay alive, to keep alerted to what they were surrounded by, to watch it even for the snake they took it to be or that larger bird they had to be in awe of, the zopalote who fed on them when they were dead or whom they looked at of a morning in a great black heap like locusts tearing up a deer had broken his wind or leg in the night. Or even Venus they watched, as though they were a grackle themselves and could attack her vertically in her house full of holes like a flute through which, they thought, when she had the upper hand she spread down on them, on an east wind, disease and those blows on their skin they call granitos. When she was new, when she buzzed the morning sky, they hid in their houses for fear of her, Shoosh Ek, for fear of her bite, the Wasp she was, the way she could throw them down like that electrical stick which, last year, pinched one of these fishermen on his cheek, in all the gulf hit him as he sat in the prow of his cayuco with a line out for dogfish of a day and laid him out dead, with no more mark burned on him than that little tooth of a kiss his wife was given as cause when they brought him out over the beach as he might have hauled in a well-paying shark.

Or to be a man and a woman as Sun was, the way he had to put up with Moon, from start to finish the way she was, the way she behaved, and he up against it because he did have the the advantage of her, he moved more rapidly. In the beginning he was only young and full of himself, and she, well, she was a girl living with her grandfather doing what a girl was supposed to be doing, making cloth. Even then he had the advantage of her, he hunted, instead, and because he could hunt he could become a humming-bird, which he did, just to get closer to her, this loveliness he thought she was and wanted to taste. Only the trouble was, he had to act out his mask, and while he was coming closer, one tobacco flower to another toward the house, her grandfather brought him down with a clay shot from a blow gun. And sun fell, right into moon's arms, who took him to her room to mother him, for she was already ready to be a wife, a man's second mother as a wife is in these parts where birds are so often stoned and need to be brought back to consciousness and, if they have their wings intact, may fly away again. As sun was. Only he could also talk, and persuaded moon to elope with him in a canoe. But there you are: there is always danger. Grandfather gets rain to throw his fire at them and though sun converts to turtle and is tough enough to escape alive, moon, putting on a crab shell, is not sufficiently protected and is killed.

Which is only part of it, that part of it which is outside and seems to have all of the drama. But only seems. For dragon-flies collect moon's flesh and moon's blood in thirteen hollow logs, the sort of log sun had scooped his helpless runaway boat out of, thinking he had made it, had moon finally for his own. Foolish sun. For now here he is back again, after thirteen days, digging out the thirteen logs, and finding that twelve of them contain nothing but all the insects and all the snakes which fly and crawl about the earth of man and pester people in a hot climate so that a lot die off before they are well begun and most are ready, at any instant, for a sickness or a swelling, and the best thing to do is to lie quiet, wait for the poison to pass. For there is log 13, and it reveals moon restored to life, only moon is missing that part which makes woman woman, and deer alone, deer can give her what he does give her so that she and sun can do what man and woman have the pleasure to do as one respite from the constant hammering.

But you see, nothing lasts. Sun has an older brother, who comes to live with sun and moon, and sun has reason soon to suspect that something is going on between moon and the big star, for this brother is the third one of the sky, the devilish or waspish one who is so often with moon. By a trick, sun discovers them, and moon, dispirited, sitting off by herself on the river bank, is persuaded by the bird zopalote to go off with him to the house of the king of the vultures himself. And though a vulture is not, obviously, as handsome a thing as the sun, do not be fooled into thinking that this bird which can darken the sky as well as feed on dead things until they are only bones for the sun to whiten, has not his attractions, had not his attractions to moon, especially the king of them all. She took him, made him the third of her men, and was his wife.

But sun was not done with her, with his want of her, and he turned to that creature which empowered her, the deer, for aid. He borrowed a skin, and hiding under it – knowing as hot sun does the habits of vultures – he pretends to be a carcass. The first vulture comes in, landing awkwardly a distance off, hobbles his nervous way nearer until, as he is about to pick apart what he thinks is a small deer, sun leaps on his back and rides off to

Olson's *casa* in Lerma, Yucatan, viewed from the beach. The house is to the left of the palm trees. Photograph courtesy of Bryant Knox.

where moon is. He triumphantly seizes her, only to find that she is somewhat reluctant to return.

At which stage, for reasons of cause or not, sun and moon go up into the sky to assume forever their planetary duties. But sun finds there is one last thing he must do to the moon before human beings are satisfied with her. He must knock out one of her eyes, they complain she is so bright and that they cannot sleep, the night is so much the same as his day, and his day is too much anyhow, and a little of the sweetness of the night they must have. So he does, he puts out her eye, and lets human beings have what they want. But when he does more, when, occasionally, he eclipses her entirely, some say it is only a sign that the two of them continue to fight, presumably because sun cannot forget moon's promiscuity, though others say that moon is forever erratic, is very much of a liar, is always telling sun about the way people of the earth are as much misbehavers as she, get drunk, do the things she does, in fact, the old ones say, moon is as difficult to understand as any bitch is.

O, they were hot for the world they lived in, these Maya, hot to get it down the way it was – the way it is, my fellow citizens.

Variations Done for Gerald Van De Wiele

This poem was written in May 1956 during the last weeks of Black Mountain College when it seemed that, for every tatter in its mortal dress, the old Rector was determined to clap his hands and louder sing. This was the semester Olson brought his new wife and son to live at the college. Robert Duncan was there to hear Olson's 'Special View of History' lectures (and invite him to give them in San Francisco the following February). In the midst of all this 'glistering' activity, the poems came out: 'The Lordly and Isolate Satyrs', 'As the Dead Prey Upon Us', and Olson's greatest celebration of life, these 'Variations' on Rimbaud's 'O saisons, ô châteaux!', a poem sometimes titled 'Le Bonheur' ('Happiness'). Olson wanted the 'Variations' named for the most loyal of the dwindling number of students. Martin Duberman in his Black Mountain volume reported:

> *Gerald van de Wiele remembers that whenever he returned from one of his frequent hitchhikes to New York and started walking up the road, 'I don't believe I ever in my life felt that I belonged any place as much as I belonged at that school. I loved that place.' (pp. 406-7)*

It should be mentioned that Olson's concern for Rimbaud was not a recent thing. The first long poem he ever wrote (in 1945) was called, 'The True Life of Arthur Rimbaud'. In his autobiographical statement for Twentieth Century

Farewell party for Stefan Wolpe, Black Mountain College 1956. Photographs courtesy of Gerald Van De Wiele.

Above, from left: Joe Dunn, Ann Simone, Grey Stone, Eloise Mixon, Bea Huss, Wes Huss, Tom Field and the Huss's child, Jonathan Williams, Joe Fiore and child, Anita Landau, Tony Landeau and child, Stefan Wolpe, Charles Olson and his son, Robert Duncan and Betty Kaiser.

Right, from left: Mary Fiore, Stefan Wolpe, Gerald Van De Wiele, Jonathan Williams, Robert Duncan, the Huss's child.

VI. OUTSIDE THE BOX

Authors *(1955)* Olson listed Rimbaud with Melville, Dostoevsky and D.H. Lawrence as *'the modern men who projected what we are and what we are in, who broke the spell'* (Collected Prose *p. 207*).

1. *Le Bonheur*

dogwood flakes
what is green

the petals
from the apple
blow on the road

mourning doves
mark the sway
of the afternoon, bees
dig the plum blossoms

the morning
stands up straight, the night
is blue from the full of the April moon

iris and lilac, birds
birds, yellow flowers
white flowers, the Diesel
does not let up dragging
the plow

        as the whippoorwill,
the night's tractor, grinds
his song

        and no other birds but us
are as busy (O saisons, ô châteaux!

Délires!

        What soul
is without fault?

Nobody studies
happiness

Every time the cock crows
I salute him

I have no longer any excuse
for envy. My life

has been given its orders: the seasons
seize

the soul and the body, and make mock
of any dispersed effort. The hour of death

is the only trespass

II. *The Charge*

dogwood flakes
the green

the petals from the apple-trees
fall for the feet to walk on

the birds are so many they are
loud, in the afternoon

they distract, as so many bees do
suddenly all over the place

With spring one knows today to see
that in the morning each thing

is separate but by noon
they have melted into each other

and by night only crazy things
like the full moon and the whippoorwill

and us, are busy. We are busy
if we can get by that whiskered bird,

that nightjar, and get across, the moon
is our conversation, she will say

what soul
isn't in default?

can you afford not to make
the magical study

which happiness is? do you hear
the cock when he crows? do you know the charge,

that you shall have no envy, that your life
has its orders, that the seasons

seize you too, that no body and soul are one
if they are not wrought

in this retort? that otherwise efforts
are efforts? And that the hour of your flight

will be the hour of your death?

III. *Spring*

The dogwood
lights up the day.

The April moon
flakes the night.

Birds, suddenly,
are a multitude

The flowers are ravined
by bees, the fruit blossoms

are thrown to the ground, the wind
the rain forces everything. Noise –

even the night is drummed
by whippoorwills, and we get

as busy, we plow, we move,
we break out, we love. The secret

which got lost neither hides
nor reveals itself, it shows forth

tokens. And we rush
to catch up. The body

whips the soul. In its great desire
it demands the elixir

In the roar of spring,
transmutations. Envy

drags herself off. The fault of the body and the soul
– that they are not one –

the matutinal cock clangs
and singleness: we salute you

season of no bungling

VII. Maximus (2): Cosmology

Lecturing on *Maximus IV, V, VI* at Simon Fraser University in 1971, Jeremy Prynne wanted to make two main points: 'Firstly, that this is a noble poem. And secondly, that it is a simple one' (*Minutes* #28, p. 4). It is noble because it transcends the lyric by taking 'the whole condition of something called the cosmos into its aim'. The volume asks 'what is the condition of being that makes it possible for man to be at home on the earth... But to be at home in that larger sense is not permitted to the lyric. It is permitted only to the great epic performances' (p. 9).

That Prynne insists that *Maximus IV, V, VI* is a single poem as well as a simple one poses the problem of making a selection. But at the same time if, as he says, each of the constituent poems 'has within it the curvature of the whole of the spatial condition', then we cannot go wrong, especially if we include the three substantial 'Maximus, from Dogtown' poems that span the volume from beginning to end.

One thing that makes this volume simple is its chronological design, which also allows for odd small poems that would not otherwise count as free-standing verse. Given their place and contiguities they turn out to be among the more attractive pieces of Olson's writing, and we have made sure to include a number of them.

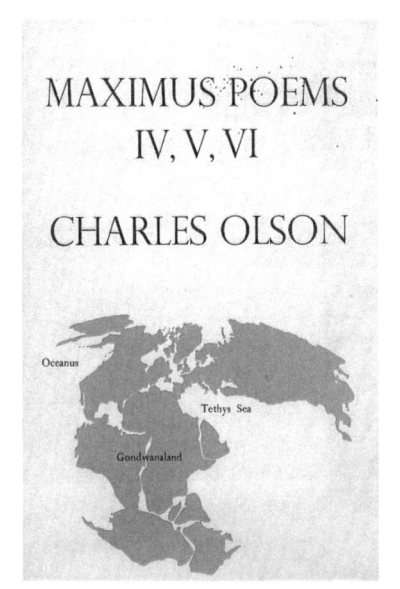

Cover of *Maximus Poems IV, V, VI* (London: Cape Goliard 1968).

Letter #41 [broken off]

Eruptions: the continents drift and collide. We all are potential volcanoes (Olson is thinking here of something Jung said). February 14, 1940: the fabled snowstorm marked Olson's leaving Gloucester's security for New York City and the greater world. And now? We are invited to ask 'What now?' as the poet places this unfinished poem at the head of Maximus IV, V, VI.

       With a leap (she said it was an arabesque
       I made, off the porch, the night of the
       St Valentine Day's storm, into the snow.
       Nor did she fail of course to make the point
       what a sight I was the size I am all over the storm
       trying to be graceful Or was it? She hadn't seen me
       in 19 years

Like, right off the Orontes? The Jews
are unique because they settled astride
the East African rift. Nobody else will grant
like he said the volcano anyone of us does
sit upon, in quite such a tangible fashion.
Thus surprise, when Yellowstone kicks up
a fuss

       Where it says excessively rough moraine,
       I count such shapes this evening in the universe
       I run back home out of the new moon
       makes fun of me in each puddle on the road.
       The war of Africa against Eurasia
       has just begun again. Gondwana

MAXIMUS, FROM DOGTOWN – I

We talk about 'the stuff of legend': the narrative core of 'MAXIMUS, FROM DOGTOWN – I' is the story of James Merry that Olson got from Edward Rowe Snow's Mysteries and Adventures Along the Atlantic Coast *(1948)*. The poem turns this legend into archetypal action, first in terms of Melville's fatal Handsome Sailor type and then, with the utilisation of Erich Neumann's The Great Mother *(1955)*, connecting the hero to the nurturing goddess and the receiving Mother Earth. A proem sets the tone by introducing Hesiod's Theogony *and* Heraclitus's Fragments.

With reference to 'my soft sow' some fifty lines into the poem: Olson never kept pigs; we must take this 'sow' in a strictly geological sense (like 'veins'). 'Sow' in the processing of pig-iron is a congealed metallic mass in a groove. It connects with the 'soft rock' of a few lines later, the permeable moraine. Both are instances of the adamantly denotative language of Olson. He was not in the habit of using casual metaphors, only the causal metaphor which turns story into myth.

proem

The sea was born of the earth without sweet union of love Hesiod says

But that then she lay for heaven and she bare the thing which encloses every thing, Okeanos the one which all things are and by which nothing is anything but itself, measured so

screwing earth, in whom love lies which unnerves the limbs and by its heat floods the mind and all gods and men into further nature

                    Vast earth rejoices,

deep-swirling Okeanos steers all things through all things,
everything issues from the one, the soul is led from drunkenness
to dryness, the sleeper lights up from the dead,
the man awake lights up from the sleeping

    WATERED ROCK
of pasture meadow orchard road where Merry
died in pieces tossed by the bull he raised himself to fight
in front of people, to show off his
                Handsome Sailor ism

died as torso head & limbs
in a Saturday night's darkness
drunk trying
to get the young bull down
to see if Sunday morning again he might
before the people show off
once more
his prowess – braggart man to die
among Dogtown meadow rocks

        'under' the dish
        of the earth
        Okeanos <u>under</u>
        Dogtown
        through which (inside of which) the sun passes
        at night –
                she passes the sun back to
        the east through her body
        the Geb (of heaven) at night

    Nut is water
    above & below, vault
    above and below
    watered rock on which
    by which Merry
    was so many pieces
    Sunday morning

<u>subterranean</u> and celestial
primordial water holds
Dogtown high
        And down
the ice holds
Dogtown, scattered
boulders little bull
who killed
Merry
       who sought to manifest
his soul, the stars
manifest their souls

VII. MAXIMUS (2): COSMOLOGY

      my soft sow the roads
of Dogtown trickling like from underground rock
springs under an early cold March moon

            or hot summer and my son
            we come around a corner
            where a rill
            makes Gee Avenue in a thin
            ford

             after we see a black duck
             walking across a populated
             corner

               life spills out

Soft soft rock
Merry died by
in the black night

fishermen lived
in Dogtown and came
when it was old to whore
on Saturday nights
at three girls' houses

Pisces eternally swimming
inside her overhead
their boots or the horse
clashing the sedimentary
rock tortoise shell
she sits on the maternal beast
of the moon and the earth

Not one mystery
nor man
possibly not even a bird
heard Merry
fight that bull by
(was Jeremiah Millett's house

Drunk
to cover his shame,
blushing Merry
in the bar
walking up

to Dogtown to try
his strength,
the baby bull
now full grown

waiting,
not even knowing
death
was in his power over
this man who lay
in the Sunday morning sun
like smoked fish
in the same field
fly-blown and a colony
of self-hugging grubs – handsome
in the sun, the mass
of the dead and the odor
eaten out of the air
by the grubs sticking
moving by each other
as close as sloths

    she is the goddess
    of the earth, and night
    of the earth and fish
    of the little bull
    and of Merry

     Merry
     had a wife

    She is the heavenly mother
    the stars are the fish swimming
    in the heavenly ocean she has
    four hundred breasts

VII. MAXIMUS (2): COSMOLOGY

          Merry could have used
          as many could have drunk
          the strength he claimed
          he had, the bravo

          Pulque in Spain
          where he saw the fight
          octli in Mexico
          where he wanted to
          show off
          dead in Gloucester
          where he did

          The four hundred gods
          of drink alone
          sat with him
          as he died
          in pieces

          In 400 pieces
          his brain shot
          the last time the bull
          hit him pegged him
          to the rock

                    before he tore him
          to pieces

                    the night sky
          looked down

Dogtown is soft
in every season
high up on her granite
horst, light growth
of all trees and bushes
strong like a puddle's ice
the bios
of nature in this
park of eternal

events is a sidewalk
to slide on, this
terminal moraine:

the rocks the glacier tossed
toys
Merry played by
with his bull

        400 sons of her only
        would sit
        by the game

        All else was in the sky
        or in town
        or shrinking solid rock

        We drink
        or break open
        our veins solely
        to know. A drunkard
        showing himself in public
        is punished
        by death

        The deadly power of her
        was there that night
        Merry was born
        under the pulque-sign

        The plants of heaven
        the animals of the soul
        were denied

Joking men
had laughed
at Merry

Drink
had made him
brave

VII. MAXIMUS (2): COSMOLOGY

Only the sun
in the morning
covered him
with flies

Then only
after the grubs
had done him
did the earth
let her robe
uncover and her part
take him in

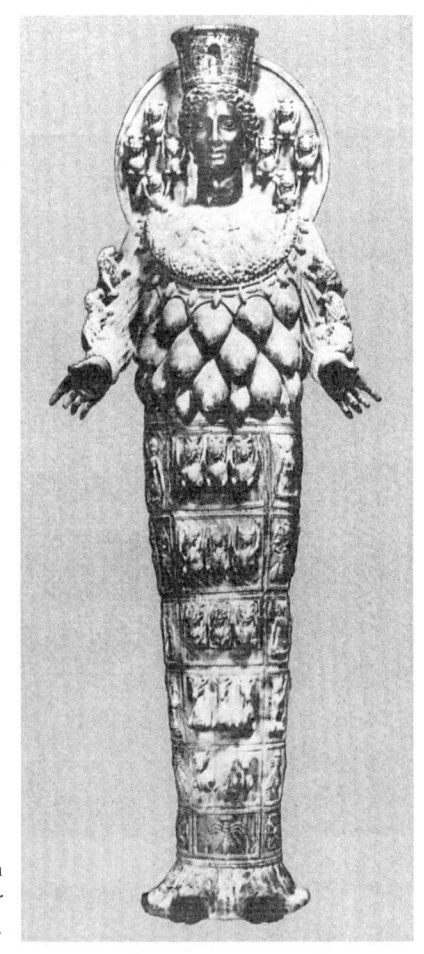

Diana of Ephesus, from Erich
Neumann's *The Great Mother*
(1955).

MAXIMUS, FROM DOGTOWN – II

There is no clearer demarcation than this poem for the change that comes into Olson's writing during Maximus IV, V, VI. *Although he names himself twice in the poem, 'Charles John Hines Ol' son' and 'Mary's Son Elizabeth's Man', any egotism has been hammered out of those words; rather it is earth, ice, stone...*

>earth is interesting:
>ice is interesting
>stone is interesting
>
>flowers are
>   Carbon
>
>Carbon is

Olson has finally achieved the 'carelessness' about himself that he had sought from the start. This is the stance toward reality he foresaw in 'Projective Verse' as proper for a nature poet, to be an object among objects:

> if he is constrained within his nature as he is a participant in the larger force, he will be able to listen, and his hearing through himself will give him secrets objects share. And by an inverse law his shapes will make their own way.

The shapes/images of 'MAXIMUS, FROM DOGTOWN – II' are obviously not directed in the normal way but are allowed into the poem, as it were, at their own demand. Readers have to draw on their 'negative capability' in order to exist among these uncertainties. One might note, however, that the Black Chrysanthemum at the end is not an extraneous horticultural decoration but was an image given Olson in an important dream recorded in the poet's notebook for 17 June 1958 (Storrs):

> Everything issues fr the
> Black Chrysanthemum
> & nothing is anything but itself
> measured so.

Olson's guide in the dream was Lü Yen, to whom is attributed The Secret of the Golden Flower: A Chinese Book of Life.

VII. MAXIMUS (2): COSMOLOGY

the Sea – turn yr Back on
the Sea, go inland, to
Dogtown: the Harbor

the shore the City
are now
shitty, as the Nation

is – the World
tomorrow unless
the Princes

of the Husting the sons
who refused to be Denied
the Demon (if Medea

kills herself – Medea
is a Phoenician
wench, also Daughter

of the Terror) as J-son
Johnson Hines
son Hines

sight Charles
John Hines
Ol'
    son

the Atlantic
Mediterranean
Black Sea time

is done in done for gone
Jack Hammond
put a stop to

surface underwater galaxy
time: there is no sky

space or sea left

earth is interesting:
ice is interesting
stone is interesting

flowers are
    Carbon
Carbon is
Carboniferous
Pennsylvania

Age
<u>under</u>
Dogtown
the stone

the watered
rock Carbon
flowers, rills

Aquarian Time
after fish
– fish was

Christ o Christ pick the seeds
out of yr teeth – how handsome
the dead dog lies! (horror X

the Migma is where the
Seeds Christ was supposed to pick out
: Wyngaershoek hoik Grape Vine HOYK the Dutch

& the Norse
and Algonquins:
He-with-the-House-on-his-Head

she-who-Lusted After-the
Snake-in-the-Pond
Dogtown berries smell

as The-Grub-Eaten-Fish-Take-the-Smell-Out-of-The
Air a e r the Ta of
Dogtown   (the Ta metarsia

    is the Angel Matter
    not to come until (rill!
    3000: we will carry water

    up the hill the Water the Water to
    make the Flower hot – Jack
    & Jill will

    up Dogtown hill on top one day the
    Vertical American Thing will
    show from heaven the Ladder

come down to the Earth
of Us All, the Many who
know
    there is One!
    One Mother
    One Son

One Daughter
and Each the Father
of Him-Her-Self:

the Genetic
is Ma the Morphic
is Pa the City is Mother-

Polis, the Child-Made-Man-Woman is
(Mary's Son
Elizabeth's

Man) MONOGENE:
           in COLLAGEN   LEAP onto
    the monogene, /in KOLLAgen   the LAND, the AQUARIAN
                                       TIME
             TIME

the greater the water you add
the greater the decomposition
so long as the agent is protein
the carbon of four is the corners

in stately motion to sing in high bitch voice the fables
of wood and stone and man and woman loved

and loving in the snow
and sun
             the weather

             on Dogtown
             is protogonic but the other side of heaven
             is Ocean

filled in the flower the weather
on Dogtown the other side of heaven
   is Ocean

Dogtown the <u>under</u>
vault heaven
is Carbon Ocean   Dogtown the <u>under</u>
is Annisquain   vault – the 'mother'
                    rock: the Diamond (Coal) the Pennsylvanian

                                    Age   the soft
                                               (Coal) LOVE

        Age   the soft (Coal love
        hung-up   burning
        under the City: bituminous

Heart to be turned to Black
Stone   the Black Chrysanthemum
is the Throne of Creation   Ocean

                         is the Black Gold Flower

The Poimanderes

A 1959 Christmas present from his friend Gerrit Lansing, Hans Jonas's The
Gnostic Religion *(Boston: Beacon Press 1958), was where Olson read the
opening lines of the gnostic text called* Poimandres *(p. 148):*

> *(1) Once, when I had engaged in meditation upon the things that are and
> my mind was mightily lifted up... I thought I beheld a presence of
> unmeasurable greatness that called my name and said to me: 'What dost thou
> wish to hear and see and in thought learn and understand?' (2) I said, 'Who
> art thou?' 'I am,' he said, 'Poimandres, the Nous of the Absolute Power. I
> know what thou wishest, and I am with thee everywhere.' (3) I said, 'I desire
> to be taught about the things that are and understand their nature and know
> God...' And he replied, 'Hold fast in thy mind what thou wishest to learn,
> and I shall teach thee.'*

> The Poimanderes: now I see what was up,
> a year ago, chomping around these streets,
> measuring off distances, looking into
> records, disconsolately
> making up things to do – finding myself peeing
> under a thin new moon on Dogtown and noticing
> rills in the March night

I forced the calm grey waters

*This poem was shaped out of 'the watery mass' with, as the poet had it in an
earlier draft (at Storrs), 'mushroom eyes'. In other words, the struggle with the
Gloucester sea-serpent of tradition was, in this instance, a by-product of Olson's
participation in two psilocybin sessions organised by Timothy Leary in December
1960 and February 1961. These sessions, however, as Olson was always at pains
to point out, did not take one anywhere but into one's essential self.*

I forced the calm grey waters, I wanted her
to come to the surface I had fought her
long enough, below. I shaped her out of
the watery mass

and the dragger, cleaning its fish,
idled into
the scene, slipped across the empty water
where I had placed
the serpent, staring as hard as
I could (to make the snow
turn back to snow, the autos
to come to their
actual size, to stop
being smaller,
and far away. The sea does
contain the beauty I had looked at
until the sweat
stood out in my eyes. The wonder is
limitless, of my own term, the compound
to compound until the beast rises from the sea.

Maximus, March 1961 – 1

A Maximus Song

This poem joins ancient legend to a modern instance, commemorating the visit to Gloucester of Timothy Leary and his family:

> *I wrote a poem on Phryne, the great mistress of Athens, walking into the sea yearly because men wished to see – men and women wished to see a perfect body. This was the model for Praxiteles' Cnidian Venus, that utterly beautiful thing. That woman, the Miss Suzanne Leary, appeared on the beach right out of this house, the front beach of Gloucester, the Pavilion Beach, at fifteen years old, and the whole town blew up at seeing a body in a bikini!* (Muthologos *1.192*)

thronged

to the seashore

to see Phryne

walk into

the water

March 6, 1961

Maximus, at the Harbor

The 'bone' which roars on to Norman's Woe in this poem is a word used for a wash of water broken into foam, usually by the bow of a ship but here by rocks fronting the tide. This violent sea must be rather like the Valentine's Day snowstorm of February 1940, accompanying a great upheaval in life or an eschatological crisis. The poem grew out of Olson's reading of Henry Corbin's 'Cyclical Time in Mazdaism and Ismailism' in Man and Time *(Eranos Yearbook 1957), which is largely to do with a concept of resurrection. That Olson turned to an angelology of this kind proposes a deep-seated need, but one we know little of, except that Ismailism appears in several poems after this as a belief system. Here is its inception in a storm where, in the middle voice construction of Greek, the phenomenon shows itself as a phenomenon (Corbin, p. 166).*

    Okeanos rages, tears rocks back in his path.
Encircling Okeanos tears upon the earth to get love loose,

that women fall into the clefts
of women, that men tear at their legs
and rape until love sifts
through all things and nothing is except love as stud
upon the earth

           love to sit in the ring
of Okeanos love to lie in the spit
of a woman a man to sit in her legs

> (her hemispheres
> loomed above me,
> I went to work
> like the horns of a snail

Paradise is a person. Come into this world.
The soul is a magnificent Angel.
And the thought of its thought is the rage
of Ocean   :   <u>apophainesthai</u>

roared the great bone on to Norman's
Woe; <u>apophainesthai</u>, as it blew
up a pool on Round Rock shoal;
<u>apophainesthai</u> it cracked as it broke
on Pavilion Beach; <u>apophainesthai</u>
it tore at Watch House Point

        II

> apophainesthai
> got hidden all the years
> apophainesthai: the soul,
> in its progressive rise
>
> apophainesthai
> passes in & out
> of more difficult things
> and by so passing
> apophainesthai
>
> the act which actuates the soul itself –
> she loomed before me and he stood
> in this room – it sends out
> on the path ahead the Angel
> it will meet
>
>   apophainesthai
>
> its ascent is its own mirage

III

The great Ocean is angry. It wants the Perfect Child.

October 23 and 24, 1961

A Later Note on Letter #15

The reality that 'Projective Verse' (1950) asked us to take a stance toward is not exactly the reality Olson sees in 1962. The attractiveness of Alfred North Whitehead's Process and Reality *(1929) was chiefly responsible for a cosmological view that might include, for instance, 'eternal events', something not dreamt of earlier. Hence the need for a new poetics.*

In English the poetics became meubles – furniture –
thereafter (after 1630

& Descartes was the value

until Whitehead, who cleared out the gunk
by getting the universe in (as against man alone

& that concept of history (not Herodotus's,
which was a verb, to find out for yourself:
'istorin, which makes any one's acts a finding out for him or her
self, in other words restores the traum: that we act somewhere

at least by seizure, that the objective (example Thucidides, or
the latest finest tape-recorder, or any form of record on the spot

– live television or what – is a lie

as against what we know went on, the dream: the dream being
self-action with Whitehead's important corollary: that no event

is not penetrated, in intersection or collision with, an eternal
event

The poetics of such a situation
are yet to be found out

January 15, 1962

'View': fr the Orontes
fr where Typhon

When Olson read this poem at Goddard College he gave some basic information: 'the Orontes River comes in at the northern end of Syria... the main manageable traffic trading outlet of the whole of the old Near East to the Mediterranean and Atlantic' (quoted in Guide, *p. 360). Besides its importance in myth, Mt Casius being the battleground of Zeus vs Typhon, the place was, in Olson's mind, the jumping off point for the whole of westward migration. In this poem we get as far as Sable Island, a landmark on the continental shelf of north-eastern America.*

        the 1st to navigate
        those waters
        thus to define
        the limits
        of the land: Helen,
        said Herodotus,
        was only the last
        of the European girls
        to be absconded with
        by the Asiatics

        for which read
        Phoenicians,
        Semite sailors

Along those extending lines (rhumbs)
there was Manes first (Minos
maybe) there had been
Gades there was Pytheas
out into the Atlantic

    far enough up into the North
    for the Atlantic to be known

        Portuguese
    are part Phoenician (?
    Canary Islanders
    Cro-Magnon

Islands,
to islands,
headlands
and shores

        Megalithic
        stones

Stations
on shores
And Sable

        Then England
        an Augustine
        land

                        January 15, 1962

after the storm was over

This précis of westward migration – with Typhon as the unnamed monster – gets us finally to Gloucester and, presumably, 28 Fort Square, which, with some difficulty, had proved big enough for Olson, his wife and son.

after the storm was over
out from his cave at Mt Casius
came the blue monster

covered with scales
and sores about his mouth
flashing not too surely

his tail but with his eyes
showing some glare
rowing out gently

into the stream, to go
for Malta, to pass by
Rhodes and Crete

to arrive at Ireland
anyway to get into the Atlantic
to make up a boil

in northeastern waters
to land in a
grapevine corner

to shake off his cave-life
and open an opening
big enough for himself

Jan 17 1962

VII. MAXIMUS (2): COSMOLOGY

3rd letter on Georges, unwritten

For a discussion of this poem, see the Introduction to this volume.

[In this place is a poem which I have not been able
to write – or a story to be called the Eastern End of
Georges, about a captain I knew about, as of the days
when it was important to race to market – to the Boston
market, or directly in to Gloucester, when she had fresh
fish, and how this man had such careful charts of his
own of these very shallow waters along the way
to market if you were coming in from the Winter Cod
Grounds on the Eastern End – the point was to cut the
corner, if you were that good or that crazy, though he
was as good as they come, he even had the charts marked
in different colored pencils and could go over those
rips and shoals dug out in a storm, driving a full-
loaded vessel and down to her deck edge, across them
as a wagon might salt licks or unship her wheels and
ferry across – it is a vision or at least an experience
I make off as though I have had, to ride with a man
like that – even have the picture of him sitting on
his cabin floor following those charts like a race-
sheet while taking the calls down the stern passage-
way and if it sounds more like Henry Ware & Paul Cot-
ter in the Eyes of the Woods, it could be so, for I've
looked & looked for the verification, and the details
of sail at a time when there were no engines – and I
went to James Connolly expecting to be able to depend
upon him, but somehow he hasn't come across, or it's
all too prettied up, and it was either Bohlin or Syl-
vanus Smith or it may have been someone as late as
Marty Callaghan but the roar of this guy going through
the snow and bent to a north easter and not taking any
round about way off the shoals to the north but going
as he was up & down dale like a horseman out of some
English novel makes it with me, and I want that sense
here, of this fellow going home]

to enter into their bodies

This poem draws on the Memphite Theology as found in Henri Frankfort's Kingship and the Gods *(1948).*

> to enter into their bodies
> which also
> had grown out of
> Earth
>
>   Mother Dogtown
> of whom the Goddess
> was the front
>
>   Father Sea
> who comes to the skirt
>   of the City

My father
came to the shore
the polyphony
came to the shore

he was as dust
in the water
the Monogene
was in the water, he was floating
away

>   oh I wouldn't let my Father
> get away
>
>   I cried out
> to my Mother
> 'Turn your head
> and quick'
>
>   & he came
> to the shore
> he came to the
> City

            oh
            and I welcomed
            him

         & was very glad

The Cow of Dogtown

This is a poem of heaven and earth. The cow of Dogtown is the sky above the part of Gloucester nearest to heaven. N.S. Shaler's 'The Geology of Cape Ann' in the Ninth Annual Report of the Geological Survey *(1889) supplied the specifics of Dogtown's earth.*

Shaler says
On Dogtown Commons
several of these areas (he is speaking of the
stratified elements of glacial accumulations
which, he has just said, generally do not rise
more than sixty feet above the sea level
/that is, now; he has already of course
made it clear that at the time the glacier
was over the land the land mass itself
was depressed from its present level by
at least double the 65 feet; which
makes it necessary to add, that, at
that same time the sea itself was 'out'
– drawn up as vapor which had else-
where formed the ice – to a depth by which the Banks,
for example, off-shore, were themselves – like
these Dogtown Commons – deposits of good
top-soil carried from other places in the feet
of the ice and only finally left – as
Dogtown and the off-shore Banks – when
the wall of the last ice began to give way)

He continues:

These elements (of glacial
accumulations) are hardly traceable in
any continuity above the level of 40
feet; but at a few points they extend
in an obscure form nearly to
the summit of the great moraines
/an example the 'top' of Dogtown,
via the Upper Road, where one comes out
(missing the Whale-Jaw) on an upland
or moor which must be about like
the barrow Bob Lowrie thinks is
a covered Viking ship
and burial. The top of Dogtown
puts one up into the sky as free-
ly as it is possible, the extent of
clear space and air, and the bowl
of the light equalling, without at all
that other, false experience of mountain
climbed, heaven. One would sit here
and eat off checker berries, and blue-
berries in season – they are around
the place, at this height,
like cups and saucers, and one moves around to
eat them, out of one's hands,
not by getting up but going from
place to place on one's own behind. Burning
balsam, or the numerous bushes of bayberry
one could stay here with the sky
it feels like as long as one chose; and
there is enough wildness, or profiles in
the rocks, the inhabitation of their shapes,
to supply plenty of company – none of the
irritation and over-presence of nothing-
nesses which makes woods, or any
place else than the kame meadows of
Dogtown and this bold height of
it, not as interesting. Shaler says: 'On Dogtown Commons
several of these areas of kame deposits
were during the period in which this
district was inhabited brought into
the state of tilled fields, and now

appear as small pasture lands destitute
of boulders.'

/This is of course identical
with Stage Fort Park, of which the
highest point is exactly Shaler's statement
of the highest of such deposits – 65'/

'These high-lying benches of stratified drift
material,' he continues, 'probably
indicate points where small subglacial
streams emerged during the process
of the retreat of the ice, bringing forth
a quantity of detrital matter and
depositing it upon the surface of the
shoved moraine at a time when the
mass lay below the level of the
sea.'

On to this kame
on to this shoved moraine
when the ice moved off
or was melted

And the land came up
and the sea rose
to the beach levels it now assumes,

and the sky
was as near, as,
at the top of the long slow rise
of either of the Dogtown roads

/or Hough avenue – or the path
from the Barrett's more steeply up to the
crown, now that Ray Morrison has cleared
away Lizzie Corliss' hen house the Barrett's
backhouse Lizzie's sad pear trees
Viola's true rubbish heap flower garden/
the far sky is as near as you stand,

Nut is over you
Ptah has replaced the Earth
the Primeval Hill
has gone directly
from the waters
and the mud
to the Cow of Heaven
the Hill stands
free

She leans
from toe to tip of hands
over the earth,
making the Cow-sign
with the earth

(she is the goddess
of earth and heaven and sea)

one could live in the night
because she has to do with it,
encompasses it
in the day on Dogtown the day
is as close as the sky

her air
is as her light
as close
one is not removed even in passing through

the air, moving around, moving from one place
to another, going even across the same field

                Nut is in the world

                              Monday February 11th, 1963

Nut supported by Shu, and the sun in its course.

Gylfaginning VI

This origin myth from Snorri Sturluson's Prose Edda establishes the Norse theme in Maximus IV, V, VI.

>   a cow Audumla,
>   which had come into being to provide food
>   for Ymir, licked a <u>man</u> /not a
>   iotunn/ out of ice whose name was
>   Buri, whose son (or maybe it was <u>B</u>urr himself)
>   Burr (or Borr) is the <u>f</u>ather of Odin

All night long

'*The initiating priests and priestesses, the hierophants and hierophantides of Eleusis, belonged to the race of the first mystery priest Eumolpos and were looked upon as his descendants: Eumolpidae*' (C. Kerenyi 'The Mysteries of the Kabeiroi' in The Mysteries *(Eranos yearbook 1955), p. 52.)*

        All night long
        I was a Eumolpidae
        as I slept
        putting things together
        which had not previously
        fit

[MAXIMUS, FROM DOGTOWN – IV]

Olson's early acquaintance with Jane Harrison's Themis *(1927) gave him a firmly rooted sense that the Olympians were not much better than hepped-up humans and that the really useful gods were those associated with annual fertility, who might fail in cosmic tragedy unless restored to power. 'MAXIMUS, FROM DOGTOWN – IV' can be taken as an attempted restoration of Typhon, fighting for his father against Zeus and the old guard, the post office bosses. The poem can be enjoyed as an idiosyncratic rendition of Hesiod's story of the battle. O'Briareos is then from Ireland?*

    a century or so before 2000
    BC |
          the year rebegan in

    March |
          festival days
of wild untamed undomesticated hence wild
savage feral (Father's
Days our father who is also in
Tartaros chained in being
kept watch on by Aegean-
O'Briareos whose exceeding
manhood (excellent manhood
comeliness

and power – 100 or possibly
to us the term of change (with
the reciprocal 1/137 one of the two
pure numbers out of which the world
is constructed
                (the other one is
'Earth' mass mother milk cow body
demonstrably, suddenly, <u>more</u>
primitive and universal (? Hardly

The problem here is a non-statistical
proof: Earth 'came into being'
extraordinarily early, #2
in fact directly following on
appetite. Or
as it reads in Norse
hunger, as though in the mouth
(which is an occurrence, is 'there',
<u>stlocus)</u>

      that the Earth
was the condition, and that she
there and then was the land, country
our dear fatherland the Earth,
thrown up to form a cairn, as spouse
of Uranos: a i a
      the original name
of Colchis (cld be a 'local'
reference, that the Great Name
the Earth shall have been
Kuban where those
inventors of the Vision – the
Civilizers – were
'local'? some sure time prior to
2000
BC
        the statistical
    (stands)
outside
the Stream, Tartaros
is beyond

the gods hunger outside
the ends and sources of Earth
        Heaven Ocean's
Stream: O'Briareos
helped out by Poseidon by being given
Cymopolea, P's daughter, for
wife, sort of only superintends
the other two jailers of those
tied up in
Tartaros – and those two,
in other words below below – below
is a factor of being, <u>underneath</u>
is a matter this is like the vault
              you aren't all train
of Heaven it counts
if you leave out those roots of Earth
which run down through Ocean to
the ends of Ocean as well
the foundations of Ocean

          – by Earth's prompting
and the advice of Heaven, his grandparents, this person
Zeus put the iotunns those who
          strain
        reach out are
         hunger
put em outside (including the last
the youngest child of Earth
her last one, by love of Tartaros,
by the aid of Love as Aphrodite made
strength in his hands and untiring
feet – and made of all the virtues
of Ocean's
children – snakes a hundred heads
(a fearful 'dragon') dark flickering tongues
the eyes in his marvelous heads flashed
'fire', and fire burned from his heads
when he looked (at the enemy or
as Shakti was shooting
beams of love directly
into the woman he wanted to be

full of love) and there are 'voices'
inside all his dreadful heads
uttering every kind of sound (imaginable?
unspeakable Hugh White says Hesiod
says (not to be voiced?

  for at one time they made sounds
  such as solely the gods
  caught on to

but at another Typhon
was a bull
when letting
out his
nature, at another

  the relentless lion's
heart's sound

  and at another sounds
like whelps, wonderful to hear
and again, at another, he would hiss
so the sky would burn

  they threw him
into his father's
place it would take you one year
from the tossing in this direction and that before you got
to its pavement, Tartaros lies
so thoroughly out 'below' but 'outside'
(having nothing whatsoever to do with
gods or Earth's... but suddenly
a 'loss' has been suffered: Tartaros
was once 'ahead' of
Heaven was prior to
(in coming into being) this 'child'
of Earth: Tartaros
was next after Earth (as Earth
was next after hunger
itself – Typhon
was her child, by Tartaros, even if last

as Heaven was her child, first

The step back, to the seam
of the statistical Nebel
and 'End of the World' out of the union of which
by what occurrence was before
hunger – it is like Ocean
which is 9 times around
earth and sea (Heaven is 9 times
around earth and sea folding and folding
earth and sea in its backward it

wraps and wraps the consistency
of mass in until the stupid story
of earth and nature is lent
what in its obviousness and effort it
can't take time for, and makes its stories
up, temporality sifts
out of Ocean out of Ocean. was born
                      3000
(when his wife was Tethys)
daughters – Tartaros the 'prison'
beyond the gods and men beyond hunger
and the foundations of Ocean
are a seam: Cottus and Gyes,
with whom Briareos is the third 'guard'
have their dwelling
            ep' 'Okeanoio 'Themethlois
the lowest part of the bottom tithemi
θε

    Ocean deems
himself

        On that edge or place
inverted from Ocean starts
another place
Tartaros in which all
who have been by the statutory
thrown down or overthrown, are
kept watch on Night and Day

VII. MAXIMUS (2): COSMOLOGY

(Night's house is right over
their heads, in which one door
Day goes out when her mother
comes in and neither
are ever together at the same time
'at home' – Hell is just over
their heads
and so is the 'way-up', Bifrost
(Styx's house and Iris the messenger are
bungled prettinesses of this way
    this marvelous ladder the
color of all colors
back where the gods, and appetite,
and so is the way out for them,
for these imprisoned original
created – all of the first creations
of Earth and Heaven (or of Ocean and Tethys
all these instances forward of except
the official story

    Heaven himself the 2nd, Kronos
who acted for his mother in de-maleing
his father
        is in Tartaros
    away from all the gods

while the glorious allies of loud-crashing Zeus
Cottus and Gyes, and o'Briareos
guard them

    Typhon
is in Tartaros,
threatening as he did (as they had,
the last to give the gods a scare
who would have come to reign over mortals
and immortals

    the heat took hold on the dark-blue sea
when Typhon and Zeus engaged
Hell trembled, where he rules
over those who have come to him

and the <u>iotunns</u> before Typhon
locked up in Tartaros swung
from the clangor and the Earth
shaking

    he burned all the marvelous heads of the monster
and conquered him and lashed him
and threw him down in his mother,
who groaned
        and a great part of her melted
as tin does from the heat of him blasted
   where Zeus had tossed him

and then in the bitterness of his anger Zeus
tossed him into Tartaros

    The life-giving earth
had crashed around in burning
the previous time when all the land had seethed
and Ocean's streams and the sea
had boiled – and it was this 'lava'-
like which had undone the earlier
Giants because they were Earth-born
Earth's own meltedness had burned
their underpinnings and
defeated them, against Zeus's
stance
      Cottus and Briareos and Gyes
had done that day, of the Civilized War,
their turn – for the Boss

   with their missiles added to his
'bolts' they did their co-evals in, and
were the ones who chained them

(as the *Theogonia* poet says,
for all their great spirit, their
metathumos

There it was, Tartaros
which had been there as early as hunger
or at least directly after hunger & Earth
and before Love
            Yet Love
in the figure of the goddess born
of the frith from her father Heaven's
parts accompanied Tartaros
(as Night had Heaven the night
his son had hurled off his parts)

Love accompanied Tartaros
when with Earth in love he made
Typhon
            #
                                    Thus
                                    March

VIII. Causal Mythology

Olson was to give a lecture at the Berkeley Poetry Conference on the morning of 20 July 1965. There was excitement in the air, for he was flying in from Italy, having participated in the Festival of Two Worlds at Spoleto (where, it was said, he had seen Pound for the first time since their break in 1948). With a side trip to a PEN conference in Bled, Yugoslavia, and returning via Caresse Crosby's castle Roccasinibalda near Rome, Olson had been, for once in his life, a jet-setter.

Jet-lag or not, Olson set himself a most difficult task with his lecture: to make his points entirely by means of poems. The idea was that if the poems were worth anything they would create a total vision of the cosmos in a way that discursive exposition could not. He had a grid of four categories within which to place the poems, but close attention reveals that he never explains anything, even while giving a strong sense of doing so. Secretly, this is a poetry reading, a reading of four poems of which the poet is immensely proud. And just to test their worth he is interested to see if they can fill out the categories of his cosmology, to see, as he puts it, 'if by any chance the relationship of, say, the four terms to the four poems will not destroy the poems'.

Another thing Olson does not explain is the title. We should perhaps take 'Causal Mythology' at its simplest: a mythology that causes, one that motivates because it is from Cause, some greater power. Which does not have to be mystical: it can be what Robert Duncan meant when in his introduction he called Olson 'the Big Fire Source'.

from Causal Mythology

CHARLES OLSON:
You know I'm very obliged to get rid of that rap for being Zeus. I never knew I was Prometheus until now. It's a fine thing. I've been a father figure too long. [Laughter] And I've begun to suffer so completely the fate of that other fellow that what I propose to do today is to expose myself, as he was, on a rock. And, in fact, if I can accomplish anything it's simply because there's a little of my liver left from overnight, like I think his was. [Laughter]

In fact, what I would like to do, actually, is to do that sort of a thing. I mean, the announced subject was 'Causal Mythology', so obviously Mr.

VIII. CAUSAL MYTHOLOGY

Duncan has prepared me perfectly. And it's very exciting to be home here, at least it feels strange and nice to be in Berkeley this morning. Especially because so many of you here are the ones that I've lived mostly for, and with, and by, myself, and care the most for in the world.

It's very strange because I suddenly was presented to Ezra Pound two weeks ago, after twenty years. And that was like – I don't know – it was not like your father or something – it was like having an Umbrian angel suddenly descend upon you and ask you to be, and be more than, well, just what you'd like to be. It was very beautiful the way the fierceness of Pound has settled down into a voiceless thing which only responded twice to me. Once I told a story of Ed Sanders, who had a beautiful picture that Pound at eighty would have a revival of life and have fifteen further years of power. The difficulty of talking to Pound is he doesn't talk anymore. He sits in an almost catatonic fix in silence. And the one word he said after I said that Sanders had that sense of him, he said, 'Sanders has a sense of humor.' [Laughter]

The thing that I *would* like to do instead of what sounds like a subject like 'Causal Mythology' is actually to talk four things:

  The Earth
  The Image of the World
  The History or City
and The Spirit of the World

and do those four things under an epigraph which would be:

  that which exists through itself is what is called meaning.

And the reason why I say that is the desire to suggest that the four terms that I am proposing are – the Earth itself, for example, is curiously today a thing which can be seen for itself. And I think that that's so completely changed the human species, literally, that it's almost like the old blessing of the pope, that it is an *orb* – and, in fact, I likewise am pairing the city, which if you remember in his blessing was the *urbs*, as that pair. And the other pair I'd like to call instead, in Latin, the *imago mundi* and the *anima mundi*. And in doing this I would like to use four poems: they're four poems written, in fact, in a run, and I'll read them not that way but read them in a series, and see if by any chance the relationship of, say, the four terms to the four poems will not destroy the poems. These will all be from the *Maximus*, written about a year ago. Some have been published. The first one is an attempt, actually a further attempt to speak my own sense at that date of the condition of the earth.

Astride
the Cabot
fault,

one leg upon the Ocean one leg
upon the Westward drifting continent,

to build out of sound the wall
of a city,

      the earth
rushing westward 2'
each 100
years, 300 years past
500 years
since Cabot, stretching
the Ocean, the earth

going NNW, course due
W from north of the
Azores, St. Martin's
Land,

      the division
increasing yet the waters
of the Atlantic
lap the shore, the history

of the nation rushing to melt
in the Mongolian ice, to arrive
at Frances Rose-Troup Land, novoye

Sibersky
slovo,

      the Wall
to arise from the River, the Diorite Stone
to be lopped off the Left Shoulder

  Now deliberately I'd like to go over it, almost like an exegesis of text, if you'll excuse me. As I said, I have arrived at a point where I really have no

VIII. CAUSAL MYTHOLOGY

more than to feed on myself. Unfortunately I didn't bring a *Maximus Poems*. Would anybody have one? That I could borrow? Thanks. I'd like very much to literally do a – for example that 'Francis Rose-Troup Land,' and that 'Mongolian ice' stuff, I'd love to just talk about the Earth in these terms. I did do an earlier passage on this particular English woman historian in a poem called 'Letter, May 2, 1959' – I'll pick a section out of it: 'then to now nothing/ new' – that would be from the seventeenth-century persons referred to just previously:

> then to now nothing
> new, in the meaning
> that that wall walked
> today, happened a bull-
> dozer discloses
> Meeting House Hill
> was a sanddune under
> what was valued for
> still the sun makes
> a west here as on
> each Gloucester hill
> why one can say what
> one can't say is
>
> when did the sea so
> roll over as later
> the ice this stuck-out
> 10 miles Europe-pointing
> cape, the lines of force
> I said to her as of Rose-
> Troup go to as one line
> as taught as uroboros ar-
> row hooped crazy Zen arch-
> er fact that arm of bow Frances
> Rose-Troup English maiden
> lady told this city what

And then it goes on into what she told Gloucester about how persons first got there. Now this thing goes on to – well, let me read that, because that is my point of the relevance of taking the Earth as a *One* – by the old law that a one is only so if it produces a one. This would be, then, if you talk a Causal Mythology, the simplicity of the principle 'that which exists through itself is what is called meaning' will be that one produces a one. The Earth, then, is conceivably a knowable, a seizable, a single, and *your* thing. And yours as a single thing and person yourself, not something that's distributed simply because we are so many and the population is growing, or that the exploitation of the earth itself is increasing.

>   ... fact that arm of bow Frances
>   Rose-Troup English maiden
>   lady told this city what
>
>   marchants Weymouth Port Book
>   No. 873 if East and West the
>   ship first employed was,
>   the date everything that
>   the local get off it Glous–
>   ter the old railroad joke
>   from the smell, the lovers
>   in the back seat the conductor
>   waking up from a snooze don't
>   look out the window sniffs
>   and calls out gloucester glous–
>   ter   All off
>
>>   Take the top off
>>   Meeting House Hill
>>   is 128 has cut it
>>   on two sides
>>
>>   the third
>>   is now no more than
>>   more Riverdale
>>   Park
>>
>>   and the fourth?
>>   the west?
>>   is the rubbish
>>   of white man
>>
>>   Up River,
>>   under the bridge
>>   the summer people
>>   kid themselves

VIII. CAUSAL MYTHOLOGY

      there's no noise,
      the Bridge
      's so high.
      Like hell. The Diesels
      shake the sky

                  clean the earth
                  of sentimental
                  drifty dirty
                  lazy man:

                  bulldozer,
                  lay open
                  the sand some sea
                  was all over the
                  second third fourth
                  meeting house,

                  once. I take my air

where Eveleth walked
out the west
on these hills
because the river

it's earth which
now is strange The sea
is east The choice Our backs
turned from the sea but the smell

as the minister said
in our noses
I am interfused
with the rubbish

of creation I hear
the necessity
of the ludicrous reference to Wm Hubbard by the
tercentennary preacher that

> the finny tribe come easily
> to the hook
>
> Fishermen
> are killers Every
> fifty of 'em I pick off
> the Records seek
> the kame I was raised
> on and are startled,
> as I am, by each granite
> morraine shape   Am in the mud
> off Five Pound Island
> is the grease-pit
> of State Pier...

And so forth. So I'm really suggesting how much this poem, which was written in '59, is very loaded, again, simply because, say, I find myself constantly returning to that unit, Earth as orb, as though it was as familiar to me as the smallest thing I know, and it's really, actually, to suggest that if there is any legitimacy to the word that we call mythology it is literally the activeness, the possible activeness and personalness of experiencing it as such.

By the way, I'd be happy to be interrupted on any of each one of these four parts this thing will constitute itself as. At the moment I'm running part one out. But I'd be happy to be picked over by anybody that wants, who is unfamiliar or is unsatisfied with any of either the information or this other thing that I'm trying to do, which is the connectivity of same to other poems of the *Maximus* at least.

BOBBIE CREELEY:
What do you mean by 'the Diorite Stone lopped off the Left Shoulder'?

OLSON:
Yeah. That I would like, Bobbie, to hold a little back because of the fourth of the – I do have a board, don't I?

(1) THE EARTH –	ORB ⎤	TRADE, UGLY, RATIONAL
(2) IMAGO MUNDI		ENYALION, BEAUTY IS WAR
(3) HISTORY –	URB ⎦	POLITICS, POLIS – JOHN WANAX
(4) ANIMA MUNDI		IKUNTA LULI – WOMAN

Can everybody see that?

The first poem that I read is called 'Astride the Cabot Fault.' I learned that, by the way, luckily in Vancouver, from one of the Vancouver people that I think isn't here today, Dan McLeod. He showed me in Vancouver a thing which I had never realized, that there's a split in the Atlantic Ocean, a fault which runs just where all my own attention has been – northeast – and that she runs right straight through Gloucester. This was, for him, very exciting. It's again, like, by the principle of the *imago mundi* or the Prometheus figure, you get stuck with all this stuff. I wouldn't propose what I'm proposing to anybody because you end up obviously being eaten by Zeus' eagle only, and you're nobody, you're not even a hero. You're simply stuck with the original visionary experience of having been *you*. Which is a hell of a thing. [Laughter] And, in fact, I assume that the epigraph that I've offered today is my only way of supporting that, which is: *that which exists through itself is what is called meaning*. All right?

I don't have any trouble stealing that, as Duncan never has any trouble stealing because he has original experience which prompts him to reach out for just what he knows he wants. I was very lucky once to have what poets call visions. And they're not dreams, as several superb poets in this room know. They are literally either given things or voices which come to you from cause. I won't quote, as one never does, one's own secrets, that's why you steal from others. But this one is an awfully good duplication. And the reason, Bobbie, I'd like very much to wait, I'm going to spend some time in this fourth thing on the poem from which I myself steal that, which is 'The Song of Ullikummi.' Actually it comes to us as a Hittite version of a Hurrian myth. It's called 'The Song of Ullikummi.' And it's the story of how this aborted creature, whom the poem calls the Diorite Stone, started growing from the bottom of the sea, and grew until he appeared above the surface of the water and then, of course, attention was called to him and he continued to grow and he became so offensive to the gods, and dangerous, that they had to, themselves, do battle with him. 'The Song of Ullikummi' is actually the story of that battle and who could bring him down. Because he had a growth principle of his own, and it went against creation in the sense that nobody could stop him and nobody knew how far he might grow. It's a marvelous Hesiodic poem. In fact, I prefer it to those passages in Hesiod that include the battle of Zeus with the giants and eventually with Typhon, because this creature is nothing but a blue stone, and the *stone* grows. I would hate to start talking mythology so much as to mention that American Indians, the Sioux, for example, believe that a stone is – I mean that Crazy Bear or something whichever was the old guy that said it, but he does say that the stone is the truest condition of creation, that it is silence and it is solidity and all that. Well, I like that. I mean, I think the Earth is nothing but a pebble, a marvelously big stone. Big Stone. Why not? Let's call the Earth 'Big Stone.' And the Diorite, for me, this Diorite figure is the vertical, the growth principle of the Earth. He's just an objectionable child of Earth who has got no condition except earth, no condition but stone. And, as you know, in alchemy this is great stuff, the lapis and all that, but one of the reasons why I'm trying to even beat the old dead word 'mythology' into meaning is that I think that it holds more of a poet's experience than any meaning the word 'mysticism' holds. The principle would seem to be that the only interest of a spiritual exercise is production.

BOBBIE CREELEY:
What's the 'lopped off the Left Shoulder'?

OLSON:
Yeah. Well this is how he finally was destroyed. I've forgotten which one of the younger gods, but it would be a character again like Prometheus, who finally took on – the old boys couldn't handle it, the women were all upset. That was cutting out, by the way, organic principles. Biomorphism is absolutely knocked flat by this figure. I mean, we don't need any longer to put up with that business, if you could get this guy back in business. Nor do we need to put up with Zeus, either, and those big-shot figures. This young other guy, like Enki or some crazy fisherman type person, finally goes down – just like, by the way, in that beautiful early, the other poem which I still respect from prehistory is the Gilgamesh story, and here it's the opposite way. And I think we live in a time when the future lies as much in the genetic as it does in the morphological. I just happen to be a form-ridden cat myself, but I respect all that action, the other side of the whole. The right arm I respect as much as my own disabled left. I wish also today to read – well I might do that right now, as a matter of fact. Let me read you another story. I'd like to read stories today anyhow. But I'd like to read a very beautiful little story about the condition of the two angels:

> He who succeeds in leaving this clime enters the climes of the Angels, among which the one that marches with the earth is a clime in which the terrestrial angels dwell. These angels form two groups. One occupies the right side: they are the angels who know and order. Opposite them, a group occupies the left side: they are the angels who obey and act. Sometimes these two groups of angels descend to the climes of men and genii, sometimes they mount to heaven. It is said that among their number are the two angels to whom the human being is entrusted, those

who are called 'Guardians and Noble Scribes' – one to the right, the other to the left. He who is to the right belongs to the angels who order; to him it falls to dictate. He who is to the left belongs to the angels who act; to him it falls to write.

And, again, I mean, I wasn't as pat as to realize I was going to read a first passage loaded on the Earth. But, again, it is why when I talk more 'intellectually' about mythology I use a word, 'dipolar.' Well, this double that we're talking about is where this Earth thing seems to me to yield. Again the Diorite Stone is the, sort of the, child of mother Earth, dig? I want, actually, to end by reading a poem I read, unhappily I guess, because nobody else said a word, in front of Ezra Pound two weeks ago, in honor of him. It fell dead, and I'd like to read it to you today as the last poem. It's on the nature of the assault upon the rock that fathers and mothers us all, sort of thing. And it's a slipped piece of the whole story – it's from 'The Song of Ullikummi.' In fact, I read it as a translation, trying to honor the fact that I thought Mr. Pound really, justly, freed the languages of the world. It's interesting to me because it is a translation from Hurrian into American. Obviously that would interest me to succeed in doing that. So that 'the Wall/to arise from the river, the Diorite Stone/to be lopped off the Left Shoulder' would be the, the fact – again let me go back, let's be really pedantic and do this. The wall of the city – 'to build out of sound the wall/of a city,' right? In the earlier second poem. 'The Wall/to arise from' – the Wall here is capitalized – 'the Wall/to arise from the river, the Diorite Stone/to be lopped off the Left Shoulder.' In fact, as I remember – I may be clear inventing – but, as I remember the Hittite Hurrian myth, it turns out, eventually, that the damned thing that grew up was actually nothing but a carbuncle on the left shoulder – like of Atlas, but of the Earth. I mean that this thing just rose, this blue stone just rose like a skyscraper and overtopped the walls of the gods. So that they were frightened it was all going to topple down on them. As indeed I am that neo-capitalism as well as communism is going to do that to the Earth.

I steal that phrase 'neo-capitalism.' I don't know it as American jive. I was quite interested in a communist poet that read – in fact, I gave the stage to him in Spoleto – Pasolini, a young Italian poet. And it's very jivey talk, apparently, in Italy today, because Italy is like ourselves; it's jumped into that new gear. Don't mind my talking history and politics currently, because we have an objection to you, Allen, Wieners and I. Because when we flew into Rome we said, 'Why don't those sons-of-bitch poets tell us how exciting experiences are?' Like just how exciting it is to fly into a city. Not that you haven't, but as a matter of fact we used you, as so many people do as a target of objection. Because you don't tell us all these wonderful things, like the condition of a poet like Pasolini, talking with his *claque!* breaking up a whole damn reading in honor of Ezra Pound, rushing out and having a press conference. It was one of the worst things I've seen. Typical lousy job! [Laughter] But the poem he read had this very exciting phrase – calling the whole present shove that's on, 'neo-capitalism.' It sounded marvelously true. It seems just what has happened in the last ten years. The whole world has [slaps his hands] done that big push that we call the species. But I'm old-fashioned enough to be – not scared – to wish that the earth shall be of another vision and another dispensation. And not from the past but from the future. OK. I didn't mean to make a pitch.

OK. I'm going to quit this Earth thing as part one, now. Jeez, I better, unless somebody wants anything more on that one poem? OK.

Now, my argument would be, then, that the way that the Earth gets to be a pea is that we are born, ourselves, with a picture of the world. That there is no world except one that we are the picturers of it. And by the world here I don't mean the Earth, I mean the whole of creation. I don't know enough, but I think that the phrase *imago mundi* is as legitimate as the better known phrase *anima mundi*. And I'd like to oppose that, really, to a condition of writing which is based on what I do or what others do, rather than comes from the darkness of one's own initiation. Again I'm suggesting that even the overt spiritual exercise of initiation is initial in us. *We* are, *we* are spiritual exercise by having been born. And that this involves one in something which Blake alone, to my mind, has characterized. He, in one passage, I've forgotten where, says that there's the ugly man, who would be the rational one; that there's the strong man, who would be wholly strong; that there's the beautiful man; and the fourth. And that these form the Son of God. I think I have that reasonably right.

And in the period, the day after I wrote this poem I read you first, I wrote this other poem. And it was refused by *The Paris Review*, so I'm happy to read it. It's never been in print. It also is a footnote, like it's an example of another side of the literal study of mythology, which I spend a lot of time on, which is really archaeology on one side or etymology on another. I found that in Crete, or in Greece at the time of Mycenae and Pylos and Tiryns, that the god who we know as Ares or Mars was apparently called Enyalios. In this poem I abuse his name by using Enyalion. But the poem is based on the word Enyalion. And it's directly connected now to the struggle of the *imago mundi*, as a child of Earth, with the bosses.

I published a long poem in *The Psychedelic Review* – due to Allen. I was brought into that early mushroom experience and *The Psychedelic Review* was one magazine that issued from it – and in order to, almost to put another kind of a plant in there, I put this poem. Literally, it led Ed Sanders to ask me to translate Hesiod. But I told him I knew no Greek, it was just cribbed from a good translation of Hesiod. But it does have that big war there between Zeus and the giants. And this starts from that, this is a later poem coming from there.

           rages
        strain
     Dog of Tartarus
   Guards of Tartarus
Finks of the Bosses. War Makers

                        not Enyalion. Enyalion
has lost his Hand, Enyalion
is beautiful, Enyalion
has shown himself, the High King
a War Chief, he has Equites
to do that

          Enyalion
is possibility, all men
are the glories of Hera by possibility, Enyalion
goes to war differently
than his equites, different
than they do, he goes to war with a picture

   far far out into Eternity   Enyalion,
the law of possibility, Enyalion

the beautiful one, Enyalion

who takes off his clothes

wherever he is found,

on a hill,

in front of his own troops,

in the face of the men of the other side, at the command

of any woman who goes by,

and sees him there, and sends her maid, to ask,

if he will show himself,

to see for herself,

if the beauty, of which he is reported to have,

is true

he goes to war with a picture

       she goes off

in the direction of her business

  over the city over the earth – the earth

is the mundus brown-red is the color

         of the brilliance

          of earth

he goes to war with a picture in his mind
that the shining of his body

    and of the chariot
    and of his horses
    and of his own equites
  everyone in the nation of which he is the High King

he turns back

into the battle

       Enyalion

is the god of war the color

VIII. CAUSAL MYTHOLOGY

of the god of war   is beauty

                 Enyalion

is in the service of the law of the proportions

of his own body   Enyalion

                but the city

is only the beginning of the earth   the earth

is the world   brown-red is the color of mud,

                         the earth
shines
          but beyond the earth

                  far off Stage Fort Park

       far away from the rules of sea-faring   far far from
                                   Gloucester

far by the rule of Ousoos   far where you carry

the color, Bulgar

              far where Enyalion

       quietly re-enters his Chariot   far

by the rule of its parts by the law of the proportion
                         of its parts

    over the World   over the City   over man

That seems to say what the image of the world, at least for me, has been.
    I can, therefore, move, I believe, to what I there call history. And I'm happy to use the word to stand for city. I mean, I'm nuts on numbers because it seems to me I'm a literalist. And I wished only to bracket these

two, say, and these two hooked obviously by words alone. [Joins *imago mundi* to *anima mundi* and *orb* to *urb*] I mean the city of the earth, which as far as I know on this continent arose in Massachusetts, and was, as you all know, quoted by... in fact, the only time I found Mr. Kennedy interesting, verbally, was when he made his appearance, just after his successful election, before the General Court of Massachusetts. I don't know how many of you would have known that he, immediately after his victory, came to, appeared, and made a speech before the General Court of Massachusetts and quoted that remarkable phrase of Winthrop's: 'that this colony shall shine like a city on a hill.' I may garble it, but some of you that know the speech may remember it. That's the one time I was moved by Mr. Kennedy. And a day after this previous poem I wrote this one. And I would like to use it to – I mean I'm excited by this series of four poems. They represent for me an outbreak of much that the *Maximus* had been approaching for me for the ten, fifteen previous years.

>   7 years & you cld carry cinders in yr hand
>   for what the country was worth broken
>   on the body
>   on the wheel of a new
>   body
>   a new social body
>
>   he was broken
>   on the wheel   his measure
>
>   was broken   Winthrop's
>
>   vision was broken he was broken the country
>
>   had walked away
>   and the language
>   has belonged to trade or the English
>   ever since   until now once more J W
>
>   can be said to be able
>
>   to be listened to: wanax
>
>   the High governor

VIII. CAUSAL MYTHOLOGY

    of Massachusetts   John

    wanax who imagined

that men

cared

for what kind of world

they chose to

live in

    and came here seeking

    the possibility: Good News

    can come

    from Canaan

And now, if I believe that these two things are mundane and these two are the realer things, I'd like finally to end with the spirit of the world, which I have never been able to see as other than the figure of woman as she is such in the very phrase *anima mundi*. I will just read this fourth poem, fifth actually of the days that these poems were written, which is the translation I promised of this section from 'The Song of Ullikummi.' For those of you who heard the poems I read in Vancouver, some of which have appeared in print since, the poem has also a connection previously. It would be impossible, I think, to read the actual transliteration. I'm actually translating the very first tablet of 'The Song of Ullikummi.' It opens up on Kumarbi, father of all the gods:

Of Kumarbi, father of all the gods, I shall sing.

Kumarbi wisdom unto his mind takes,
and a bad 'day,' as evil (being) he raises.
And against the Storm-God evil he plans,

And against the Storm-God a *rebel* he raises.

Kumarbi wisdom unto his mind [takes],
And like a bead he sticks it on.

When Kumarbi wisdom unto his mind had taken,
from (his) chair he promptly rose.
Into (his) hand a staff he took,
Upon his feet as shoes the swift winds he put.

And from (his) town Urkis he set out,
and to *ikunta luli* he came.
And in *ikunta luli* a great rock lies:

And that's where I picked it up.

    fucked the Mountain
    fucked her but good   his mind
    sprang forward
and with the rock he slept
and into her he let his manhood
      go   five times   he let it go
                ten times   he let it go

         in ikunta luli   she is three
     dalugasti long
            she is one and a half
    palhasti wide. What below she has
up on this his mind sprang upon.

When Kumarbi his wisdom
he took upon
his mind
      he took his istanzani
      to his piran   hattatar
      istanzani   piran daskizzi

Kumarbis -za   istanzani piran hattatar
daskizzi
       sticks wisdom
unto his mind   like his cock
into her
iskariskizzi

VIII. CAUSAL MYTHOLOGY

      the fucking
of the Mountain
        fucked the Mountain
              went right through it
                      and came out the other side

  the father of all the gods
  from his town Urkis
  he set out
  and to ikunta luli
  he came

    and in ikunta luli a great rock
    lies
    sallis perunas
    kittari   he came upon
    What below she has
                 he sprang upon
    with his mind
             he slept
    with the rock   kattan sesta
    with the peruni

        and into her   misikan X-natur
andan   his manhood
           flowed
into her

And five times he took her
nanzankan   5-anki das
and again ten times he took her
namma man zankan   10-anki das

Arunas
the Sea

    Thank you. [Applause] I see I'm short. If anybody wants any more – not any more of that! – but I mean if this lecture isn't complete I can complete it.

RICHARD BAKER:
The clock is fifteen minutes slow.

OLSON:
Oh, is it? Oh, good. [Laughter]

RICHARD DUERDEN:
Could you give a different shot at that *anima mundi* as woman, did you say?

OLSON:
Yeah, I just meant the rather classic figure which I... well, for example in the Tarot deck it's the *El Mundo*, card XXI is *anima mundi*. She's the Virgin... she's the whole works. She's it.

QUESTION:
Well, why do you go to another culture to get your myth?

OLSON:
Well, you knock me out if you say that. I just thought I bridged the cultures [Laughs] I don't believe in cultures myself. I think that's a lot of hung up stuff like organized anything. I believe there is simply ourselves, and where we are has a particularity which we'd better use because that's about all we got. Otherwise we're running around looking for somebody else's stuff. But that particularity is as great as numbers are in arithmetic. The literal is the same as the numeral to me. I mean the literal is an invention of language and power the same as numbers. And so there is no other culture. There is simply the literal essence and exactitude of your own. I mean, the streets you live on, or the clothes you wear, or the color of your hair is no different from the ability of, say, Giovanni di Paolo to cut the legs off Santa Clara or something. Truth lies solely in what you do with it. And that means *you*. I don't think there's any such thing as a creature of a culture.

I think we live so totally in an acculturated time that the reason why we're all here that care and write is to put an end to that whole thing. Put an end to nation, put an end to culture, put an end to divisions of all sorts. And to do this you have to put establishment out of business. It's just a structure of establishment. And my own reason for being, like I said, on the left side and being so hung up on form is that I feel that today, as much as action, the invention – not the invention, but the discovery of formal structural means is as legitimate as is for me the form of action. The radical of action lies in finding out how organized things are genuine, are initial, to come back to that statement I hope I succeeded in making about the *imago mundi.* That *that's* initial in any of us. We have our picture of the world and *that's* the creation.

I mean with some deliberateness I should expose myself. I shrank everything that I feel and know about mythology into those four in order to offer today, to you, at least, that best shrinkage I know at this moment. Is that fair?

I do want to, really, use that papal blessing which I still, as a Catholic, am impressed by. You do all know that, that after his election each pope is required to come to that door, in that horrible building by Michelangelo and Raphael, and bless the city and the world. And I really – I mean, that moves me, like. That's why I'd say the mundane is recognizable too. [Writes on blackboard] And the other bracket, which I do put on the left don't I, is that one.

And I don't mind proving – I mean it's fun to do this today, to take poems and do what nobody – I mean, just let them be proof. Test them as proof. I think poems and actions both should stand that. If they fall down then it's our intellectualism only that's been exposed.

Charles Olson
Causal Mythology

Cover of the Four Seasons Foundation *Causal Mythology* (1969), showing Olson at the blackboard, Berkeley Poetry Conference, July 1965.

IX. Maximus (3): Earthly Paradise

On 29 March 1964, Betty Olson, driving alone, slid off the icy road near their home in Wyoming, New York, and was killed, leaving a distraught husband and a nine-year-old son. After a while, Charles Peter went to his aunt, who was also a resident of Gloucester. Olson, in and out of hospital, kept on with his teaching at the State University and even returned to Buffalo for the following academic year, but living out of a suitcase in the motel across from the campus. In the third week of what would have been Olson's third year at Buffalo, he went out to the airport and wrote on a Mohawk airlines boarding pass to Albert Cook, the understanding chair of the English Department: '... the truth of the matter is I haven't been one hour happy or well – except literally while working – since I left home. I hope you will therefore hear me, that the only possible conceivable thing I can do seems to be to stay at home' (*Selected Letters*, p. 338).

So he returned to Gloucester, and Gloucester was his home for the remaining four years of his life. Alone in his upstairs rooms at 28 Fort Square he wrote the poems that came to comprise the posthumous *Maximus Poems Volume Three* (1975), including the great meditative poem, 'I'm going to hate to leave this Earthly Paradise', so accurate about the passage of the early hours of the night, so reassuring to the reader that the poet had made the right decision.

having descried the nation

The word 'descry' can certainly be thought of in its old perjorative sense, since 'the nation' is still the threat that Olson sees as he looks out from 'Watch House Point', the early name for his Fort Point, and the natural place on the harbour for a sentinel to be to warn and protect the city.

having descried the nation
to write a Republic
in gloom on Watch-House Point

Maximus to himself June 1964

After a bout in hospital, Olson tried living again, now alone with Charles Peter, in the house in Wyoming, New York, where the coffin of the wife and mother had been closed two months before. On the day Olson and his son visited the Gratwicks, old friends living nearby, he came home and wrote what must be one of the great short elegies of the English language, 'Maximus to himself June 1964'. The 'golden cloak' and the 'dogs' are dream material brought in from earlier poems. So too is the Lady of Good Voyage, the image of the Virgin which stands between the spires of the Portuguese church in Gloucester, holding in her arms not the Christ child but a fishing schooner, in such a way that the boats leaving the harbour can see that she has them in her care. All these things, expressed in the poem with the plaintive 'no more,' are now unshared.

>   no more,
>   where the tidal river rushes
>
>   no more
>   the golden cloak (beloved
>   World)
>
>   no more dogs
>   to tear anything
>   apart – the fabric
>
>   nothing like
>   the boat (no more Vessel
>   in the Virgin's
>   arms
>
>   no more dog-rocks
>   for the tide
>   to rush over not any time again
>   for wonder
>
>   the ownership
>   solely
>   mine

Figure of the Madonna cradling a ship, on the roof of the Portuguese church of Our Lady of Good Voyage, Gloucester, Mass. Photograph courtesy of the Charles Olson Society.

Cole's Island

Cole's Island, on the northwest outskirts of Gloucester, is not a real island, so the connotations of this poem do not lie in that direction. Given Olson's concerns at the time the poem was written, we should rather think of the Cinvat Bridge which Olson read of in Henry Corbin's 'Cyclical Time in Mazdaism and Ismailism' in Man and Time *(Eranos Yearbook 1957). Corbin speaks of how 'eternal Time can be apprehended as a celestial Person' (p. 137). One is 'incarnated as an earthly human soul whose celestial counterpart is the Soul of Light or Angel which it encounters "on the way" to the Cinvat Bridge, which separates the two universes'. This encounter 'signifies the shift of limited time to eternal Time; the attainment of Destiny itself and the plenitude of the Light of Glory' (p. 142). This Angel seems quite heavily disguised in the poem, but the shift out of the ordinary could be akin, knowing what was in Olson's mind, to Corbin's summary: 'while one is materially present in this world, there is a mode of being in Paradise' (p. 165).*

IX. MAXIMUS (3): EARTHLY PARADISE

I met Death – he was a sportsman – on Cole's
Island. He was a property-owner. Or maybe
Cole's Island, was his. I don't know. The
point was I was there, walking, and – as it
often is, in the woods – a stranger, suddenly
showing up, makes the very thing you were do-
ing no longer the same. That is suddenly
what you thought, when you were alone, and
doing what you were doing, changes because someone else
shows up. He didn't bother me, or say anything. Which is
not surprising, a person might not, in the circumstances;
or at most a nod or something. Or they would. But they wouldn't,
or you wouldn't think to either, if it was Death. And
He certainly was, the moment I saw him. There wasn't any question
about that even though he may have looked like a sort of country
gentleman, going about his own land. Not quite. Not it being He.

A fowler, maybe – as though he was used to
hunting birds, and was out, this morning, keeping
his hand in, so to speak, moving around, noticing
what game were about. And how they seemed. And how the woods
were. As a matter of fact just before he had shown up,
so naturally, and as another person might walk
up on a scene of your own, I had noticed
a cock and hen pheasant cross easily the
road I was on and had tried, in fact,
to catch my son's attention quick enough for him
to see before they did walk off into the bayberry
or arbor vitae along the road.

               My impression is we did –
that is, Death and myself, regard each other. And
there wasn't anything more than that, only that he had appeared,
and we did recognize each other – or I did, him, and he seemed
to have no question
about my presence there, even though I was uncomfortable.
    That is,
Cole's Island
is a queer isolated and gated place, and I was only there by will
to know more of the topography of it lying as it does out
over the Essex River. And as it now is, with no tenants that one

                                                               can speak of,
it's more private than almost any place one might imagine.
And down in that part of it where I did meet him (about half way
                                                          between the
two houses over the river and the carriage house
at the entrance) it was as quiet and as much a piece
of the earth as any place can be. But my difficulty,
when he did show up, was immediately at least that I was
an intruder, by being there at all
and yet, even if he seemed altogether
used to Cole's Island, and, like I say, as though he owned it,
even if I was sure he didn't, I noticed him, and he me, and he
went on without anything extraordinary at all.

Maybe he had gaiters on, or almost
a walking stick, in other words much more
habited than I,
who was in chinos actually and
only doing what I had set myself to do here
& in other places on Cape Ann.

    It was his eye perhaps which makes me
render him as Death? It isn't true, there wasn't anything
that different about his eye,
    it was not one thing more than that he was Death instantly
that he came into sight. Or that I was aware there was a person
here as well as myself. And son.

    We did exchange some glance. That is the fullest possible
account I can give, of the encounter.

                                        Wednesday, September 9th, 1964

Maximus of Gloucester

'The monks who built the abbeys of Cluny and Saint Denis took no thought of money, for it regarded them not. Sheltered by their convents, their livelihood was assured, their bread and robe were safe; they pandered to no market, for they cared for no patron. Their art was not a chattel to be bought, but an inspired language in which they communed with God, or taught the people.' Brooks Adams The Law of Civilization and Decay *(1943 edn, p. 347).*

    Only my written word

    I've sacrificed every thing, including sex and woman
    – or lost them – to this attempt to acquire complete
    concentration. (The con-
    ventual.) 'robe and bread'
    not worry or have to worry about
    either

    Half Moon beach ('the arms of her')
    my balls rich as Buddha's
    sitting in her like the Padma
    – and Gloucester, foreshortened
    in front of me. It is not I,
    even if the life appeared
    biographical. The only interesting thing
    is if one can be
    an image
    of man, 'The nobleness, and the arete.'

    (<u>Later</u>:   myself (like my father, in the picture) a shadow
               on the rock.

                                     Friday November 5th 1965

[to get the rituals straight

That Maximus has by this time become Charles Olson makes no difference: with the walls down, he cannot help but be, as the previous poem had it, 'an image of man'.

[to get the rituals straight I have

been a tireless Intichiuma eater & crawler of my own

ground until I went today from

John & Panna up where Gloucester thins out

home, & feeling
    what a small-town a dug-out I am

descending into, & have lived in as my pit

as, by Riverdale mills I

was again wakened as that

Indies captain had his Chinese boat

on Mill pond I heard my own

gnawing comed out & rituelle

Sabéen mine
       actually ismaël-
   lienne

        topi animated until

even the Earth 7,500,000 years off us

is my

gravel

IX. MAXIMUS (3): EARTHLY PARADISE

Sunday

night June 19th with some hope my own daughter

as well as 3 year old Ella may

live in a World on an Earth like this one we

few American poets have

    carved out of Nature and of God

        [and son for that matter but I was thinking of swinging

        – or push me like Ella said on my swing]

    Love makes us alive   The careful ones I care for are those few

                people – John Wieners,

                Edward Dorn & the women they love,

        and Allen Ginsberg in some way at least
which in a poem like The Telephone or his unbelievable ability to
                              make a picture
                  postcard alive front & back
or even a beer coaster or a photograph taken by himself

              and Robert Creeley of course who like I is tight
                              where lusimeles goes

having written to Joyce

Benson 2 or 3 days ago that those poets whose

mental level does permit them to

know order, is <u>for</u>

    participation mystique   the

                  paths (Intichiuma

                          made known,

                                            Love made known

                                                        MDCCCCLXVI

Celestial evening, October 1967

In this poem Olson is remembering a passage from Hesiod's Theogony *(Loeb, pp. 135–7):*

> *Far under the wide-pathed earth a branch of Oceanus flows through the dark night out of the holy stream, and a tenth part of his water is allotted to her [Styx]. With nine silver-swirling streams he winds about the earth... but the tenth flows out from a rock, a sore trouble to the gods.*

Olson imagines this tenth stream of Oceanus as flowing into our interior being and acting something like it did for the gods: detecting lies and deceits, for which we, like the Olympians, may suffer ostracism.

        Advanced out toward the external from
        the time I did actually lose space control,
        here on the Fort and kept turning left
        like my star-nosed mole batted
        on the head, not being able to
        get home 50 yards as I was
        from it. There is a vast

        internal life, a sea or organism
        full of sounds & memoried
        objects swimming or sunk
        in the great fall of it as,
        when one further
        ring of the 9 bounding
        Earth & Heaven runs

IX. MAXIMUS (3): EARTHLY PARADISE

into the daughter of God's
particular place, cave, palace – a tail

of Ocean whose waters then
are test if even a god
lies will tell & he or she spend
9 following years out of the company
of their own. The sounds

and objects of the great
10th within us are
what we hear see are motived by
dream belief care for discriminate
our loves & choices cares & failures unless
in this forbidding Earth & Heaven by

enclosure 9 times round plus
all that stream collecting as,
into her hands it comes: the

full volume of all which ever was which we
as such have that which is our part of it,
all history existence places splits of moon
& slightest oncoming smallest stars at
sunset, fears & horrors, grandparents'
lives as much as we have also features
and their forms, whatever grace or ugliness our legs
etc possess, it all
comes in as also outward leads
us after itself as though then
the horn of the nearest moon was
truth. I bend my ear, as,
if I were Amoghasiddi and,
here on this plain where
like my mole I have
been knocked flat, attend,
to turn & turn within
the steady stream & collect which
within me ends as in her hall and I

hear all, the new moon new in all
the ancient sky

*Added to making a Republic

Obviously attached to the earlier 'having descried the nation', this poem draws on the message that Olson got from Pound in a dream (Guide, p. 712):

> of rhythm is image
> of image is knowing
> of knowing there is
> a construct

though the Confucius quotation is added from another source, The Secret of the Golden Flower *(1931 edn, p. 37).*

*

Added to

making a Republic

in gloom on Watchhouse

Point

    an actual earth of value to

    construct one, from rhythm to

    image, and image is knowing, and

    knowing, Confucius says, brings one

    to the goal: nothing is possible without

    doing it. It is where the test lies, malgre

    all the thought and all the pell-mell of

    proposing it. Or thinking it out or living it

    ahead of time.

Reading about my world,
March 6th, 1968

I'm going to hate to leave this Earthly Paradise

That this piece was sent out by Olson for publication (it appeared in Stony Brook *1/2 [Fall 1968]) is evidence that the poet stood by what might seem to some to be ramblings through the early hours. Olson was overwhelmingly a night person; what we have here represents, perhaps more than anything else he wrote, the truth of his working life in these last Gloucester years. The elongated phone call was to Harvey Brown, prompted by his gift of S.H. Nasr's* Science and Civilization in Islam *(Harvard University Press 1968), which Olson had started reading on 31 July 1968. He had marked a passage on the Muslim prophet Idris and the possible contact between Muslim and Chinese science:*

> *the word* al-kimiya *from which 'alchemy' is derived, is itself an arabization of the classical Chinese word* Chin-I, *which in some dialects is* Kim-Ia *and means 'the gold-making juice'. (pp. 31–2)*

The poem is the alembic process as far as Olson, the adept in his night watch, was able to further it.

Mary B. Mellen, *Moonlight on a Bay* (Gloucester Harbor, 1870s; formerly attributed to Fitz Hugh Lane). Copyright © Shelburne Museum, Shelburne, Vermont.

Interior of 28 Fort Square, c. 1968. Photograph courtesy of the Charles Olson Society.

Charles Olson's kitchen table, 1968. Kate Olson Archive.

IX. MAXIMUS (3): EARTHLY PARADISE

    I'm going to hate to leave this Earthly Paradise

                             (Monday August 5th
                           – at post 1:10 AM (of
                        the 6th) having finished
              (at 1:10) the longest telephone call
              I believe I ever did have –
              since <u>before</u> 9 PM ? to
                      1:10 AM?
              4 plus hrs? to one
              person?

    this alembic of the strongest (when
    Mauch Chunk, P. A. is changed to Jim
    Thorpe, P. A. – and Mollie McGuires are filmed
        in such re-al-it-y

The earth is dug down to low – Lane
cldn't paint it but he understood, es-
pecially in full moonlight or near full though
equally it is true in the day when
the tide is all the way out there
is at the shore – boats hanging
over on their side rock shapes con-
forming to another shore the
points of land encompassing more
– reaching out further embracing more
roughly gauntly milder water breaking
more loudly in the stillness lower
Earth makes water louder un-
familiar grounds and islands
– 10 Lb Island enormous in the
height so severely suddenly ac-
quired Dunkums Point & Rocks
as if tonight Lane himself were
painting Moonlight on the
At Low Water Harbor
Scene: I said to my friend my
life is recently so hairy honkie-

hard & horny too to that ex
tent I am far far younger
now than though of course I am
not twenty any more, only
the divine alone interests me at
all and so much else is other-
wise I hump out hard &
crash in nerves and smashed
existence only

such a night or the recent day a
low tide then over Harbor Cove flashed
in my eye as though a vessel was
(in fact it was on the railway
there) up on the land so low lay
now that urban destruction has
permitted the Atlantic Halibut wharf
to turn to concrete rubble all
of Duncan Point is bush & rock &
weed, a view too Lane was
interested in as he spotted
a single red flower on the low tide's edge &
I that am over on any Dunkums
Federal Rubbish picked vetch
& took it to the Diner asking
the new summer waitress please
for a 2nd glass of water glass for
it I didn't know was vetch but
flowering weed: low tide night is
just the same the bright white moon
light slashing harbor water as
differently in look & sound as
waters noises coming up beside

this Ragged Arse Rock Earth
                    divine
upon such August low tide night
I celebrate what Fitz Hugh Lane
                    too
                    saw

IX. MAXIMUS (3): EARTHLY PARADISE

hobbling about like cats & I on
his weed-crippled legs on <u>his</u> side of
the same shore I look out full on the
Harbor, Lane Hawthorne's
sweet contemporary when Noah Webster
was their senior & the earth had not
yet known its etymology yet he
as Hawthorne had the emotions
Shiva meant when war was nec-
essary even against the Goddess of the
Three Towns herself in
the crumpled dirty wild Tripura
Earth & Sea themselves supply when
moon & sun draw tides so far
Shiva had to draw his bow to kill
Tripura 'cause
    why other than that man & gods
                         alone
                        betake
a day or time when only only <u>one</u>
& 4th condition God himself makes
necessary to a vision I no more than Lane
can give the art to though
in day or night I know tonight the rubble
I'll be free to cut away like nails
of all my toes and fingers maybe
too in pain to see the Earth
dug down again

        ?Monday Aug 5th
        – 2AM plus
        (of the 6th)

pre-Testament & Muslim Arabian pre-Phoenician
holy Idris view of lowest Trismegistus
take anything but one thing only out of
coffee human being or visit talk or work
one element of all a low tide night or day

teaches me is Enoch's view here
for Fitz Hugh Lane's clumsiness of
foreground in so many paintings I
have cut off at my loss & now
this night regain the virtue of
in loneliness & in such pain I can't
lift the bottom of the alemb the gold-
making juices lie in sounding in the
striking of the surf & waves while
off-shore out the Harbor for the 1st
of all the nights of life I've lived upon,
around this Harbor I hear also
even in the fair & clear near round
& full moon August night the
Groaner and the Whistling Buoy in their
soft pelting of the land I love
      as though I were my love & master Bach
and say in hymn & prayer
himself
      God festen Berg or Earth Is Shown
      Beneath Her Nails tonight.

                O., for Lane, in
             hymn & celebration
          of Idris   Ragged Arse Gloucester
                                       and
      the Everlasting only worth the life
                                2:25 AM

burning gold water-strip setting
even-sided to my feet like Robeson Channel
marking Wegener Fault the full length of the
Western Harbor to Fort Point from near full
moon setting this date in the West as far
south as to sink tonight exactly in
the Cove of Freshwater Cove as red or
fire or orange or of gold-water as
Al' Idris is in the Chinese
word of Al' chimiya   Al' chimiya the
Gold-making machine I sd disclosing
myself in bungling it repeating it to
Harvey Brown two hours ago

IX. MAXIMUS (3): EARTHLY PARADISE

                    2:45 Aug
                5 (6th   'LXVIII

with all the new bright lights which make
Natalie Hammonds 17th century fake
Dollivers neck a Sausalito Over the Bay
in now Modern post pre-literate Am-
america (same day minutes later

        plane overhead & whiting vessel's
                                  going
too fast as the school bell rings the hours too
fast over on Wonsons Paint Manufactory at
point above Black Rocks on Rocky Neck

                     – just rang
                              Two Bells for
            what goes out an hour between
            2 and 3?

              Flying Saucer landing, Blinking Lights, Beverly
                                      Force Base?
                  Air Port possibly or Hanscom Air

             moon go down   mad lumpy upper

       shape like two nights ago 3/4

       pushed-in left-side face like

       Frank Moore's birth face forceps
            bent

                 salmon-pink glow now

              as school bell will
              in two minutes ring
                3 o'clock in the morning

The first of morning was always over there

Completing the circle of a personal uroboros, Olson could look from his kitchen window across the beach to Stage Fort, where he had played every summer of his childhood and where he returned in college vacations to work as a substitute letter carrier.

The first of morning was always over there,

and, when I went to work, to be at the Post Office

at 7:15 – or 7:25, and before 7:30, the

Cut was so often a pleasure to walk,

hurriedly yet likewise Harbor air gulls

already bummaging – and freshness I only

look at now. Or can feel, like this morning,

in my kitchen at even an earlier hour, eating

probably already poisonous Pacific waters (in Geisha crab-meat

& drinking the juice with pleasure) pride in love

lending my blue robe even firmer feeling that

even Genji and/or Lady Murasaki couldn't

even in that far distant & more heightened time

have been more relaxed in their hands and

fingers or more alert to morning's

beginning even though their duty & life

lifted toward a more caparisoned day

than I shall already lying back here in bed

again to sleep Sunday away, my own life &

nerves having day & night as parquet or

Go-board for my less lucid & wilder

American-Chinese millennium to live in

Sunday morning, April 20th
'LXIX

I live underneath the light of day

Among the papers brought by Olson from Gloucester to the University of Connecticut in his last forage into the world were pages torn from Johannes Brøndsted's The Vikings *(Penguin Books, 1960). Preserved in the Olson Archive at Storrs they reveal in marked passages what this poem is about in its inception:*

> Another runic inscription, cut on the underside of a slab covering a grave of about a century before the Viking Age at Eggjum in Sogn (Norway), declares that neither stone nor runes have ever been exposed to sun's light and that the runes were not carved with an iron knife. In other words: both stone and runes are dedicated in secret to the dead man and to none other. This, the longest of all the early inscriptions, commands further that the stone must never be brought out into the light of day. (pp. 195–6)

In the first lines of the poem Olson's heaviness feels to him like the stone slab of this passage; or he himself is as good as buried with the inscription above him. But then he throws off such feelings and thinks of the long stone walls of the Connecticut countryside, megaliths that take him back to Hesiodic origins and then finally forward to 'another kind of nation'. The text breaks off without elaboration, except he has already placed before us, by fragmentary allusion, a quotation from Jung's Psychology and Alchemy, *p. 25: 'Through time and exact definition things are converted into intellect.'*

I live underneath
the light of day

    I am a stone,
or the ground beneath

My life is buried,
with all sorts of passages
both on the sides and on the face turned down
to the earth
or built out as long gifted generous northeastern Connecticut stone walls
                                                                    are

through which 18th century roads still pass
as though they themselves were realms,

the stones they're made up of
are from the bottom such Ice-age megaliths

and the uplands the walls are the boundaries of
are defined with such non-niggardly definition

of the amount of distance between a road in & out
of the wood-lots or further passage-ways, further farms
are given

        that one suddenly is walking

in Tartarian-Erojan, Gaean-Ouranian
time and life love space
      time & exact
analogy time & intellect time & mind time & time
spirit

            the initiation

        of another kind of nation

X. Appendix: 'Maximus, to himself'

'Maximus, to himself' was the poem that Charles Tomlinson chose for the 'Black Mountain Anthology' in *The Review* No. 10 (January 1964), and it has been a favourite anthology piece since. When Gerard Malanga came to Gloucester to interview Olson for *The Paris Review* in April 1969 (a few months before Olson's death) he asked if the poet would read 'Maximus, to himself' onto the tape. Olson began to comply, but broke off to make comments which are both a retraction and an affirmation. This Appendix extracts the main flow of that part of the transcribed conversation.

It is pertinent that an early version of 'Maximus, to himself' in the Olson Archive at Storrs is in the form of a dramatic monologue, in the conventional sense of being ascribed to a historical personage, in this case, of course, Maximus of Tyre. The draft, presented here in facsimile, is close to the final version but has interesting variants.

On Olson's kitchen table during the interview was a copy of *The Park* 4–5, a magazine that had arrived that day from England, containing a review of *Maximus IV, V, VI* by Jeremy Prynne, from which Olson quotes with some excitement.

TYRE

"I have had to learn the simplest things,
last. Which makes for difficulties.
Even at sea I was slow,
to get the hand out or to cross
a wet deck. The sea was not, finally,
my trade, but even my trade, at it,
I stood estranged
from that which was most
familiar - delayed, and not content
with that man's argument:
that such postponement
is now the nature of
obedience, that we are all late,
that we grow up many,
and the single
is not readily
graspED.

"It could be. Though the sharpness
I note in others makes more sense
than my own distances, the agilities
they show daily who do the world's
business. And who do nature's
as I have no sense I have done,
either.

   I have made dialogues,
discussed ancient texts, thrown
what light, offered
what pleasures doceat
allows. But the known - this,
I have had to be given,
a life, love, and from one man,
a world. Tokens. But sitting here,
I look out as a wind and water, testing -
and missing
some proof.
   I know the quarters,
but the universe of it, the direction,
this, still, I took from their welcome,
or their rejection,
of me. And my arrogance
was neither diminished,
nor increased,
by the communication.

It is undone business I speak of
this morning
with the sea stretching out
from my feet.

X. APPENDIX: 'MAXIMUS, TO HIMSELF'

from 'Paris Review' Interview

'Maximus, to himself' is like a soliloquy; it has the lesion of talking about myself, which I permit myself at this one point at all seams – and it's only two I've written so far do you permit yourself to let the leak in. Otherwise, the boundaries have to be as tight as our structural – our 'moral structures.' I can read this, I hope. And it's sort of like – the first sentence, which is so boring. I mean:

> I have had to learn the simplest things last.

I mean, it's so bad don't ever have anything to do with it. It's one of them truths that, if you can avoid, for god's sake avoid, because I can assure you, like fifteen years later, don't listen to me. [LAUGHS] 'I have had to learn the simplest things last.' I told Harvey Brown's wife today I'm still only catching up with – as a matter of fact, I've gone all to pieces backwards, because the simplest is going to occur tomorrow. What am I going to do? [LAUGHS]

> Which made for difficulties.

Hm-m.

> Even at sea...

Well, this is now interesting. I mean, that's where I really was a dope. I was with men who moved in their environment, and I was from another environment. And I don't mind. I told you that story of being in a restaurant in Gloucester this week, and feeling every bit of the movement of my position... I mean, this cat today, like he say: 'He was pretty wary in that first book of the sea, what?' Oh, what a gracious statement! 'At the same time, very often fulsome.' But this is where I'll be, like, very wary.

Or I can read a new poem! May I? Like, a brand new poem – on this same subject. Just one minute, then I'll go on. [GETS MANUSCRIPT]

> 'Her stern –'

Hm. I'm talking about the same thing – and I'll come back to this slowness on the deck – the same ship, same vessel, same sea – like any place today where there's action, god help us:

> Her stern like a box the
> *Doris Hawes* waddled
> off Brown's out of the offshore westerly until
> after the lightning storm I thought
> shall she never come back from the oasis
> of the full North Atlantic its-
> self?

It seems like the whole truth to me, that this beautiful little vessel, which brrrrrrr going to the eastward, you know, to get out of the storm, and I'm brrrrrerrerr. There the lightning, berrberber. And I'm thinking as I wrote this poem – I just got so excited. I don't know whether it makes it, like, but you can hear the levin, I mean, the absolute pratfall, beluaaah! Will she ever get her stern out of the full North Atlantic in some way? Come on, come on, come on out of it!

Yeah. 'I was slow to get the hand out.' That's obvious. Also: 'To cross a wet deck.'

> The sea was not, finally…

That sounds awfully stupid: perfectly obviously not.

> But even my trade, at it, I stood estranged…

Woo-er. That's very clumsy. I couldn't make it at all. And I don't care about being 'delayed,' and all that argument. Bullshit. No. No envy of 'who do the world's businesses.' Bullshit. Now…

> I have made dialogues

(That's true.)

> I have discussed ancient texts

(To my pride.)

> have thrown what light I could.

I think that's a little bit special pleading… it's begging your sympathy… please. But I'd thought, like, I'd change the syntax, it would be OK:

I've discussed ancient texts;
on some things have been original, innate, inertial,
never to be forgotten.
Fuck you.
Can't do it again.
Somebody can.... .

And 'offered what pleasures doceat allows.' Which is what, like, I'm stuck with. I mean, when he says 'moral,' oh my christ, I'm with him entirely. It's the one thing I marked: 'moral structure of immediate knowledge.' That's doceat! That's all it is, that's what's called 'teachings.' And either you do it or you don't, and it's a wide open choice. And I don't see why anyone would do it, because, my christ, I mean, it so both infines and confines your existence that you just have to have existence... This is where his knowledge gets to all those as Europeans, whom I love, my beloved, my beloved former nation. And what I would wish I lived in today, simply because of the grace of life, which is still yours, my dear Europe, as against this abusive, vulgar, cruel, remorseless and useless country, the United States of America. May she perish in these five years, simply not because of any radical wish at all, but that she would get out of our way, and leave us alone, and leave things alone which she has harmed and harmed and harmed. And for what? For nothing. For something which she herself no longer values, and will buy her nothing. And immediately, redemptorily, we will all be in the same boat with all the leaks of this filthy system, which has purchased all of our lives at its cost. Not really, thank god, god damn her soul, because she didn't have enough strength to win us... This country has been unconscious. And it's got to awake. That's my belief, and it's why I've spent so much time just, like, painting her dales and sails and seas or something. I mean, you can't do anything but be the piper of a sleeping nation.

OK, excuse me. I go back to this one. This poem is tennis. I don't like this poem. But it's also very accurate. I was absolutely physical. I could do those things, the 'agilities.' And I wasn't 'late,' to tell you the truth. That's the point, goddamnit. I didn't know enough to say, 'Look, you horse's asses, you're pullin' me back! I wanta go! I wanta go!' It only comforts people today who are sort of dragging their asses.

I don't mind. I can read it now, if you'll hear me, having done what this guy says I did, which is to move the fuckin' thing so I could talk about the weather:

> I know the quarters of the weather...

I mean, that's just so ignorant. I could've said 'the fours': the 'protein corners'

> ... where it comes from...

And where it's going ever since. Remember the way that goes: 'into the proteins of the four corners of,' huh? How about that?... It took me all these years. Whew! But I knew it instantly, by the way. There's that point. I knew this poem was no good from the moment that I wrote it. [LAUGHS] It's absolutely true. Hear me. If you don't hear this, I haven't got anything left.

Notes

I. Prologue

'La Préface' was written about 23 April 1946 (early TS at Storrs). Though it was intended for a catalogue for Cagli's show in Chicago, that printing could not be arranged, and it appeared first in *y & x* (1948), a book of five Olson poems opposite five drawings by Cagli. The *Collected Poems* text is used here.

'The Resistance' took shape from a draft letter of 13 January 1949 to Natasha Goldowski of Black Mountain College (Storrs archive). See *What Does Not Change*, p. 80. It may have been completed for Jean Riboud on the occasion of his wedding, 1 October 1949. It was dedicated to him on its publication in *Four Winds* (Winter 1953). This version, which was reprinted in *Human Universe* and *Collected Prose*, differs from the Storr TS in two significant details. The original TS has been chosen for inclusion here.

II. Parents

'The Post Office' was written February–March 1948, but remained unpublished until George Butterick's edition of *The Post Office: A Memoir of His Father* (Bolinas, California: Grey Fox Press, 1975), the text used here.

The first version of 'As the Dead Prey Upon Us' was dated 13–16 April 1956 (TS at Storrs). The version printed in *Ark II / Moby I* (1956–7) and in *Collected Poems* is used here.

III. Projective Verse

In a letter of 24 February 1949 Olson told a friend, 'I am locked in what looks like my first long poem' (*Selected Letters*, p. 93). From a mass of material that was to have been called *The Proteid*, 'The Kingfishers' was put in its final form in July 1949. It was published in *Montevallo Review* (Summer 1950) and in *Collected Poems*.

'Projective Verse' was submitted to *Poetry New York* in March 1950. They asked for revisions, which were made in discussion with Robert Creeley in correspondence. It was returned for publication in October 1950. The present text is taken from this periodical printing.

IV. Maximus (1): Polis

This section begins with four poems out of the thirty-eight which make up *The Maximus Poems* (1960).

'Letter 3' (I.9–12) was sent from Black Mountain College to Vincent Ferrini when his new magazine *Four Winds* was reviewed badly in the *Cape Ann Summer Sun* for 18 July 1952. It was revised in April 1953 for publication in *Four Winds* 2/3 (Fall–Winter 1952–3).

'The Songs of Maximus' (I.13-16) were sent from Washington DC to Vincent Ferrini in Gloucester for *Four Winds* 4 (Winter 1953).

'Letter 10' (I.45–7) was written at Black Mountain College, but was sent straight to Jonathan Williams for *Maximus 1–10* around 1 May 1953, there being no time for prior periodical publication.

With 'Capt Christopher Levett (of York)' (I.133–5) Olson is resident in Gloucester. On 20 February 1958 he bought Charles Herbert Levermore's *Forerunners and Competitors of the Pilgrims and Puritans* (1912), which reprints Levett's *Voyage into New England, 1622–24*. The poem was written at this time, though not printed until the 1960 *Maximus* volume.

The additional poem, from *Maximus IV, V, VI*, is 'Maximus to Gloucester Letter 27 [withheld]'—'withheld' from the 1960 collection, that is. It was published in the *Yale Literary Magazine* (April 1963), and then in the second collection (II.14–15).

V. In Thicket

We use here a facsimile of 'La Chute' as sent to Frances Boldereff on 25 May 1949 (*CO/FB*, p. 37). It was published in *Goad* (Summer 1951) and *Collected Poems*.

The first draft of 'In Cold Hell, in Thicket' was sent to Frances Boldereff on 23 May 1950 (*CO/FB*, p. 347). It was revised the next day and sent off to a Japanese periodical, but it was apparently not printed until *Golden Goose* (Series three) #1 (1951). The *Collected Poems* text is used here.

We know that 'The Ring of' was sent to Robert Creeley in a letter of 11 October 1951, which has unfortunately not survived. The poem was published in *In Cold Hell* (1953) and *Collected Poems*, the text used here.

VI. Outside the Box

Part 1 of 'The Gate & the Center' was drawn from a letter to Robert Creeley dated 27 July 1950 (*CO/RC* 2.81–4) and part 2 from one dated 4 August 1950 (*CO/RC* 2.92–5). At Creeley's suggestion Olson stitched the two pieces together, reworked them and sent him the result on 18 October 1950. Cid Corman accepted the essay for the first issue of *Origin* (April 1951). This text, which appears in *Human Universe* and *Collected Prose*, has been amended here in a few places by collation with the original letters.

When Robert Creeley came to edit *Selected Writings of Charles Olson* (1966) he included *Mayan Letters* complete; it is almost irresistible not to follow suit, but space considerations determined that about half the letters could be used here, taken from Creeley's text. The full body of the letters that comprise *Mayan Letters* can now be perused in volumes 5 and 6 of the *Complete Correspondence* of Creeley and

Olson from Black Sparrow Press, and the efficacy of Creeley's selection for *Mayan Letters* approved.

The poem 'To Gerhardt, There, Among Europe's Things...' is dated in the text: 'June 28th, '51, on this horst on the Heat Equator,' i.e. Yucatan. It was first published in *Origin* 4 (Winter 1951–2), the text used here.

The first draft of the 'Human Universe' essay was finished in Mexico and sent to Cid Corman on 17 June 1951; it appeared in *Origin* 4 (Winter 1951–2) after revision in line with suggestions from Robert Creeley in correspondence. The text as it appears in *Human Universe* is here amended in two places where the typescript supplies corrections.

'Variations Done for Gerald Van De Wiele' was written at Black Mountain College in early May 1956 and published in *Measure* 1 (Summer 1957), also in *The Distances* and *Collected Poems*.

VII. Maximus (2): Cosmology

Maximus IV, V, VI was to have come out from Jargon/Corinth like the 1960 predecessor, and it was actually in page proofs by June 1966 when a spate of letters to Eli Wilentz and Jonathan Williams reveals Olson's revulsion at the type font and leading. He ultimately withdrew the book and, after seeing the production values of *'West'* that Goliard Press did for him in London, he confidently put the volume into the hands of Tom Raworth and Barry Hall. Hence its appearance in November 1968 under the Cape Goliard imprint.

'Letter #41 [broken off]' (II.1) was written March 1959. This, as many of the poems of *Maximus IV, V, VI*, did not have prior periodical publication.

'MAXIMUS, FROM DOGTOWN – I' (II.2–6), dated in MS 20 November 1959, was first published as a pamphlet by Auerhahn Press in 1961.

'MAXIMUS, FROM DOGTOWN – II' (II.9–10) was first published with the title 'December 5, 1959', in *Sidewalk* 1:1 (Edinburgh) in 1961, and subsequently in *Paris Review* 37 (Spring 1966).

'The Poimanderes' (II.17) is from a reading of Hans Jonas's *Gnostic Religion*, which Olson read on 5 February 1960.

'I forced the calm grey waters' (II.32) is dated March 1961.

'A Maximus Song' (II.35), dated 6 March 1961, was published in *Set* 1 (Winter 1961–2).

'Maximus, at the Harbor' (II.70–1) is dated 23–4 October 1961. The last line does not appear in the first printing in *12 Poets & 1 Painter Writing* 3 (1964).

'A Later Note on Letter #15' (II.79) is dated 15 January 1962.

'"View": fr the Orontes...' (II.81) is dated 15 January 1962.

'after the storm was over' (II.94), dated 17 January 1962, was published in *The Nation* 197 (7 December 1963).

'3rd letter on Georges, unwritten' (II.107) was meant, if written, to go in the sequence at a point early in 1962. The prose note that it became was probably a last minute effort before *Maximus IV, V, VI* went to press.

Notes in Henri Frankfort's *Kingship and the Gods* indicate that the poem 'to enter their bodies' (II.147) was written 26 January 1963.

'The Cow of Dogtown' (II.148–150) is dated 11 February 1963.

'Gylfaginning VI' (II.155) – exact date of writing not known, but the sequence would indicate February 1963.

'All night long' (II.157) was written early March 1963.

'[MAXIMUS, FROM DOGTOWN – IV]' (II.167–72) was written March 1963 and first published in *The Psychedelic Review* 1:3 (1964).

VIII. Causal Mythology

Donald Allen was immediately alert to the usefulness of this lecture of 20 July 1965 and, receiving the tape recording from Berkeley Audio-Visual Department, transcribed it for his Four Seasons imprint as *Causal Mythology*, Writing 16, 1969. With some emendation George Butterick used this text for *Muthologos*, and with some further emendation this is the text used, in part, here. Olson's poems included are as follows:

1. *Earth* 'Astride the Cabot fault' (III.37).
   'Letter, May 2, 1959' (in part) (I.147).
2. *Imago Mundi* 'rages strain' [Enyalion] (III. 38–9). Prose from Henry Corbin's *Avicenna and the Visionary Recital* (1960).
3. *City* '7 years & you cld carry cinders in yr hand' (III.41). Olson also read 'Some Good News' (I.120) not included here, and also 'Capt Christopher Levett (of York)' (I.133) found in section IV above.
4. *Anima Mundi 'from* The Song of Ullikumi' (in *Collected Poems*).

IX. Maximus (3): Earthly Paradise

The Maximus Poems Volume Three edited posthumously by Charles Boer and George Butterick (New York: Grossman Publishers, 1975) maintains the chronological arrangement and the sense of the volume as a diary. (Olson once called these poems his 'dailies'.)

'having descried the nation' (III.9) was from June 1963 but intended by Olson for the first poem of the volume (*Guide*, p. 505).

'Maximus to himself June 1964' (III.53) is dated on the MS 4 June 1964.

'Cole's Island' (III.69–70), dated 9 September 1964, was published in *Poetry* (April–May 1965) and awarded that magazine's Oscar Blumenthal–Charles Leviton Prize.

'Maximus of Gloucester' (III.101), dated 5 November 1965, was published in the *Literary Magazine of Tufts University* 1:1 (Winter 1966).

'[to get the rituals straight' (III.173–4), dated within the text of the poem 19 June 1966, was published in *Pacific Nation* 1 (3 June 1967).

'Celestial evening, October 1967' (III.182–3), dated in the title, was unpublished in Olson's lifetime but has become something of an anthology piece.

'*Added to making a Republic' (III.190), dated 6 March 1968, was published as a small broadside by the Institute of Further Studies, 1968.

'I'm going to hate to leave this Earthly Paradise' (III.197–201) is dated to the minute throughout (the year is 1968). It was published in *Stony Brook* 1/2 (Fall 1968).

'The first morning was always over there' (III.207), dated 20 April 1969, is printed here with two emendations.

'I live underneath the light of day' (III.228) was written on a University of Connecticut notepad along with Olson's other last poems dated 23 November 1959. One emendation.

X. Appendix: 'Maximus, to himself'

'Maximus, to himself' (I .52–3) was written in April 1953, as was the draft 'TYRE'. The poem 'her stern like a box' was included in the California *Maximus Poems* (1983) by George Butterick. It was new at the time of the interview, 15 April 1969. The section of *The Paris Review* interview here transcribed was previously published in *Muthologos* 2.147–51 (with a fifth reel transcribed by Charles Watts in *Minutes* #2, pp. 28–37). Olson quotes 'protein / the carbon of four is the corners' from 'MAXIMUS, FROM DOGTOWN – II' to indicate how his poetry left 'Maximus, to himself' behind.